*For Bob,
with admiration,
Mike*

Dostoyevsky's Stalker and Other Essays on Psychopathology and the Arts

Spring 2010

Michael Sperber

D0851411

UNIVERSITY PRESS OF AMERICA,® INC.
Lanham • Boulder • New York • Toronto • Plymouth, UK

Library of Congress Control Number: 2009942079
ISBN: 978-0-7618-4993-3 (paperback : alk. paper)
eISBN: 978-0-7618-4994-0

Portions of this book have appeared in earlier versions in several journals and books over the years. Grateful acknowledgement is made to the following copyright holders:

American Imago, "Camus's *The Fall:* The Icarus Complex" (1969).
Current Psychiatry: "The Case of the Quadriplegic Cyberterrorist" (2002).
Journal of Analytical Psychology: "The Daimonic: Freudian, Jungian and Existential Perspectives" (1975).
Literature and Psychology: "Shame and James Joyce's 'The Dead'" (1991).
Provincetown Arts: "Cloaked Shame: The Mask of Terrorism," "Jo and Ed," "Thoreau's Afternoon Walk."
Psychiatric Quarterly: "Sensory Deprivation in Autoscopic Illusion" (1969).
Psychiatric Times: "Prison and the Mental Jail" (2002).
Psychoanalytic Review: "The 'As-if' Personality and Chekhov's 'The Darling'" (1971); "Thoreau's Hallucinated Mountain" (2004).

For Schatzie . . .
and for
Lisa, Raul, Paul, Jeff, and Skip:

One word frees us
of all the weight and pain of life.
That word is love.
— *Sophocles*

Contents

Preface

This collection of essays on psychopathology and the arts is based on the modus operandi of both medical psychologists and literary artists, and I pay homage to one with the following passage from his autobiography.

In his autobiography (1967), the American poet and author William Carlos Williams, a medical psychologist who practiced pediatrics, has this to say about his approach:

> My "medicine" was the thing that gained me entrance to the secret gardens of the self. It lay there, another world, in the self. I was permitted by my medical badge to follow the poor, defeated body into these gulfs and grottos. And the astonishing thing is, that at such times and in such places—foul as they may be—just there, the thing in all its greatest beauty, may be freed to fly for a moment guiltily about the room.

Dostoyevsky's Stalker and Other Essays on Psychopathology and the Arts is a report of my journeys into "the secret garden of the self," using my "medical badge" to follow "the poor, defeated" mind and spirit into the "gulfs and grottos" as a physician and teacher. After my visits into these "gulfs and grottos," I would use the great works of literature, art, and cinema to understand what I had seen and teach others what I had learned. The idea for this approach came to me as a psychiatrist working and teaching in a prison and at a university.

In the courses at the prison, I presented a study of lives to provide inmates with positive role models (e.g., Mahatma Gandhi or Martin Luther King, Jr.) or negative role models (e.g., the Unabomber or Dostoyevsky's Underground Man). In the university courses, I would present a particular psychopathological syndrome or disorder in connection with a character in a movie (e.g.,

Woody Allen's Zelig) to illustrate "identity diffusion"; or a work of art (e.g., Grant Wood's *American Gothic*) to depict a certain type of marital disharmony.

The writer, cineaste, or painter often presents vivid details of such psychological problems, arranging them in so telling a fashion that they become memorable to students—"the thing in all its greatest beauty [is] freed to fly ... about the room." Through their art, they make the world more comprehensible. This anthology considers the ways art accomplishes this, and, combining it with the approach of medical psychology, it enables readers to become participant-observers of the human heart in conflict and the sufferings of the psyche. Balance is essential: too much the observer, we are cold fish, but too participatory, we become part of the problem—and in both instances, we lose our perspective. The chapters that follow grew out of not only my presentations but a search for this balanced perspective, and their insights are a badge for all to enter "the secret gardens of the self."

Acknowledgments

Over the years, I have had the good fortune to meet a handful of people whose interest in art, music, or literature overlapped with their enthusiasm for abnormal psychology and psychiatry.

This began in high school with my English teacher, William F. Marvin, M.A., also a psychologist, who got me off to a good start. Bill would enter the classroom, smile, lean forward, wait until he had everyone's attention, and then read a poem or a short story, sometimes without even providing the author's name or the book's title.

Anton Chekhov's "Misery" comes to mind. This story is not only about the grief of a Russian sleigh-driver whose son recently died, but above all the driver's misery resulting from his futile efforts to share the heartache with his passengers, who are too busy to hear his woe.

After the long, contemplative silence usually following Bill's presentations, he would lead a lively discussion about the psychology involved—in this case, the human need to share pain. In Chekhov's story, the despair of the Russian sleigh-driver, Iona Potapov, is evident. Settled into a fetal-like position in the carriage, snow falling all about him, he is dead to the world,

> all white like a ghost. He sits on the box without stirring, bent as double as the living body can be bent. If a regular snowdrift fell on him it seems as though even then he would not think it necessary to brush it off.

At the day's end, when the driver is comforted by the horse, who seems to hear his despair, the relationship between psychology and the arts is as clear as the way cadaverous Potapov's life is restored by his little mare munching her oats, who seems to listen, breathing on his hands.

Many years later, I taught a course in Harvard's Social Relations Department, "Personality Syndromes Through Literature." Picking up where Bill left off, that course and this book are ways of expressing my gratitude—although he is long since dead.

I am also grateful to two other mentors for questions they posed, twenty years apart. In 1966, after accepting my essay "Camus' *The Fall*: The Icarus Complex" for publication in *American Imago*, Professor Henry A. Murray, eminent Melville scholar and creator of the Thematic Apperception Test, asked, "What do you think is the clinical significance of that complex?" It surprised me that the man who delineated the Icarus complex would be perplexed about its relevance.

Two decades later, I found the answer to Murray's question in another context. After a presentation to the Thoreau Society in 1982, "Thoreau and Mental Health," the leading Thoreau scholar at the time, Professor Walter Harding, told me he had culled all of Thoreau's dreams from his writings, but was baffled as to their meaning. "Do you think depth psychology can illuminate them?" he asked. We met regularly in the little house behind the church in Concord, using Walt's *The Days of Henry Thoreau*, to understand the poet-naturalist's night life.

When we came to Thoreau's recurrent "Rough-Smooth" nightmare, which he averred was like his life, "*an alternate . . . Insanity and Sanity*," it became clear to me that Thoreau had experienced bipolar (manic-depressive) disorder from his early years. Again, literature and psychology: the high-flying Icarian imagery Thoreau used is indicative of mania, and the subterranean and labyrinthine imagery, which I called Daedalian, is suggestive of depression.

It has been a delight to present insights from my essays to diverse audiences, in prisons, colleges, hospitals, and at professional conferences. Once, after a lecture at the local library on Chekhov's "The Darling," a woman introduced herself, said that she was much like its protagonist, Olenka, and wanted to make an appointment with me to discuss her problems. Subsequently she became a patient, learning much from Chekhov's insights as well as teaching me more about them. I express appreciation to her and to the many students and patients I have had who have taught me much about the human heart in conflict, the subject of so many great works of art.

With respect to *Dostoyevsky's Stalker*, I have been blessed by the contributions of a number of people. When I first washed ashore in Provincetown, Massachusetts, over thirty-five years ago, I had the good fortune to meet Christopher Busa, the versatile publisher of *Provincetown Arts*. Chris and I have shared many interests, from the drifting dunes of Cape Cod and the red clay of its tennis courts, to literature and psychology.

Through Chris, I had the good fortune to cross paths with Susanna Ralli, whose suggestions for improving the manuscript have always been perceptive and tactfully presented. Susanna noted that one of the essays which I proposed for this anthology did not belong in it. Thanks to her, I removed it and it has become the cornerstone of my fourth book, *Bartleby's Feast: Resilience versus Despair.*

Randall Conrad, *encyclopédiste*, Thoreauvian and meticulous researcher who brought me into the digital age before it was too late, toiled at the manuscript and checked the references—a heroic feat, because in many cases I did not leave him much to go on. He has been a patient and discerning editor over the years and a first-class friend.

Douglas Worth, fellow writer, musician, and spiritual ally, has explored with me most of the themes expressed in this book and provided thoughtful criticism of the final text. It is a privilege to have the ongoing warmth of his friendship and spiritual understanding.

In the end, I must assume all responsibility for any shortcomings in the book, but I wish to acknowledge my indebtedness to all who have been part of this project.

I should also like to express my gratitude to the persons named in the dedication. Lisa and Jeff, my imaginative, curious and resourceful progeny, have attended many of the movies, read many of the stories, and heard much of the music woven into these essays. I am grateful to them for their ongoing love, patience, and perceptive observations.

My older brother Skip, who has known me longer than anyone else, has done what he could to inform me of life and been a good teacher. The enthusiastic idealism of my younger brother, Paul, has been a delight. Raul, bright, unpretentious, and caring, the most recent member of our family, is already a most welcome and indispensable part of it.

For over four decades I have had the splendid good fortune to enjoy the friendship of Claude Bloch, a remarkably thoughtful and compassionate person. Claude and I have explored most of the topics discussed in this book together over the years, and I am indebted to him for many of the insights I gained during our conversations.

Schatzie, woman of my dreams from our Oberlin College days, has read every word of these essays in their various incarnations and offered wise reflections. The nickname "Schatzie" suits her well—she is a valuable treasure in every sense.

Introduction: The Relationship of Psychopathology to the Arts

Fyodor Dostoyevsky was never stalked, so far as I know, but he did have a stalker, the unnamed antihero of *Notes from Underground*. In the Underground Man's monologic harangue, which constitutes the novella, he details the process leading from a dehumanizing encounter with a six-foot-tall army officer to his obsessive pursuit of the man.

Entering a tavern one day, he inadvertently blocks the precipitous departure of the sizeable lieutenant, who lifts him bodily, and wordlessly displaces him to the side like a chair, so that he can pass. The Underground Man is mortified: "I could have forgiven even a beating, but I could never forgive his moving me out of the way and entirely failing to notice me." Soon after this depersonalizing encounter, the compulsive pursuit begins.

It is possible to schematize the pathogenesis of stalking from this account of a "small and scrawny" man, who conceives of himself as a "human housefly," with the massive military man:

The Escalating Cycle of Terrorism

Impotence & Disrespect → Mortification → Shame Rage →
Retaliation & Terrorism → Impotence & Disrespect, etc.

Retaliation leads to further impotence and disrespect, and an escalating cycle of terrorism. I confirmed this conceptualization, derived from the Dostoyevsky novella, as I was treating a cyberstalker and in a study of the Unabomber.

A psychiatric syndrome, similarly, may be delineated from Anton Chekhov's story "The Man in a Case," which applies, among others, to the musical genius Glenn Gould, who made out of his recording studio, for example, the type of encasement to which Chekhov referred.

Dostoyevsky's Stalker not only deals with the way literature provides insights for students of psychopathology, but also considers the way this discipline illuminates works of art. For example, Olenka, Chekhov's enigmatic protagonist in "The Darling," becomes less perplexing when readers learn that her imitative mode characterizes what psychoanalysts designate an "as-if" personality.

If Picasso's observation that "art is a lie that tells the truth" is accurate, the truths of the responses of Tolstoy's characters' Ivan Aksenov and Makar Semyonych in "God Sees the Truth but Waits" cast light on the psyches of their nonfictional counterparts, Alger Hiss and Whittaker Chambers. The devastating impact of mortifying shame on the psyche is evident in the psychic maelstrom in which the character Gabriel Conroy (in James Joyce's "The Dead") and Jim (in Joseph Conrad's *Lord Jim*) founder, as well as in its erosive effects on the male lovers in Annie Proulx's short story (and Ang Lee's film) "Brokeback Mountain."

Dostoyevsky's Stalker proposes a paradigm shift in psychiatry. The symptoms of mental illness may have constructive uses. Instead of seeking to remove guilt, shame, fear, or even a hallucination, for example, we may find a way to use them for mental and spiritual growth. Alexander Pushkin's story "The Shot," for example, describes the innovative way its protagonist, Silvio, transforms mortifying shame into compassion. The section "Henry David Thoreau, Mohandas Gandhi, and Martin Luther King, Jr.: Crisis, Preparation, and a Deliberative Moment" describes how stress may be used to transcend a potential destructive predicament. Similarly, Frederick Law Olmsted's early stress disorder played a role in his development of psychoarchitecture. August Kekulé's hallucinated snake mouthing its own tail led him to imagine the cyclic structure of the benzene ring and, with it, the inception of organic chemistry.

Even when growth resulting from the underlying psychopathology is not particularly impressive, e.g., as described in the section "Reinvented Selves," there is much to be learned about low self-esteem and the idealized self from such accounts as Frank Abagnale's *Catch Me If You Can* and James Thurber's 'The Secret Life of Walter Mitty."

Finally, this anthology on psychopathology and the arts, in the last section, explores the relationship between the imagery of the Greek myths of Icarus and Daedalus and affective disorder, demonstrating the way these images in Henry David Thoreau's journal and sketches cast light on his mania, depression, and bipolar states, and the way these images reveal the underlying mood disorder of Albert Camus' antihero in *The Fall*.

FOUR THEMES

I have called this book an anthology; I emphasize that it is a collection of discrete essays. These thirty-some chapters can be read (or assigned to be read) at random, as needed. For greater ease, nevertheless, the chapters have been grouped under four key themes. These categories were selected for different reasons: *shame* because of its phenomenal capacity to enhance growth; *stress* because of its ubiquity in our society; *hallucinations* because some may be useful in creativity; and the *imagery of moods* because it casts light on the underlying effects of free association, daydreams, nightmares, works of art, and literature.

The poet-physician Dannie Abse made an observation about the importance of literature for the practice of medicine: "*Literature and medicine? Almost as necessary for a medical education as a stethoscope.*" For the layperson, insightful psychological literature is as good as a prescription for a wonder drug.

Part I

VARIATIONS ON A THEME OF SHAME

Where there is no shame, there is no honor.

—African proverb

The more things a man is ashamed of, the more respectable he is.

—George Bernard Shaw

Chapter One

Shame, the "As-if" Personality, and the Search for Identity

Shame is the consciousness or awareness of dishonor, disgrace, or condemnation. It arises when there is a failure to live up to one's ego ideals. Knowledge of what shames a person provides insight into that person's value system. Whereas guilt is a painful feeling of distress about one's actions, shame targets the painful feelings about one's identity, not simply one's actions. It is the Cinderella of the emotions, often disregarded because of the discomfort engendered when the effect is invited out of the hearth's ashes into the living room.

The failure to crystallize an identity, whether spiritual, sexual, or vocational, may result in intense shame. Consider the unfulfilled talent of Patricia Highsmith's Tom Ripley, Frank Abagnale, and Henry Thoreau as a young man. All struggled with what psychoanalysts call an "as-if" personality, experiencing profound feelings of shame, in the absence of a meaningful vocational identity—a "calling."

Confusion about one's sexual identity may give rise to a profound discomfort. Consider Ennis del Mar, protagonist of Annie Proulx's short story and Ang Lee's motion picture "Brokeback Mountain," whose feelings of alienation and psychological detachment, symptoms of overwhelming shame, were somewhat less agonizing for his lover, Jake Twist, who was better able to accept his bisexual identity.

Toxic shame, the experience that leaves one feeling like a flawed or defective human being, results from a traumatic encounter with shame, such as pianist Glenn Gould's humiliation by Leonard Bernstein at the time of their final encounter. Henceforth, Gould would refuse all public performances. The tragic outcomes of James Joyce's "The Dead," Joseph Conrad's *Lord Jim*, Theodore Kaczynski ("The Unabomber at Harvard"), and "The Case of the Quadriplegic Cyberstalker" all stem from toxic shame.

Conrad's Jim, the novel's protagonist, and Tom, the antihero of Patricia Highsmith's *The Talented Mr. Ripley*, were unsuccessful in crystallizing an authentic sense of self and consequently felt mortified by shame. In expiation, Jim arranges for himself to be killed and Tom Ripley turns to serial killing.

It is possible to transcend mortifying shame and transform it meaningfully, as Gurov does in Chekhov's "Lady with the Pet Dog." Frank Abagnale, author of the autobiographical *Catch Me If You Can*, and young man Thoreau also managed to overcome the stigma, guilt, and shame that accompany failed identity.

Shame mastery requires a steadfast vision of what needs to be accomplished, uncompromising ego ideals, self-validation, and perseverance toward these goals.

IDENTIFYING THE SELF

At dinner one evening, I admired the poem of a friend who told me he enjoyed writing poetry but did not identify himself as being a poet. When I asked how he did identify himself, he was at first astonished and I asked why. "No one has ever asked me that question before," he replied. He thought a moment and then answered, "I think that I would say I was a fortunate person."

This time I was the astonished person. I had never before heard someone identify him- or herself by a state of mind. People usually describe themselves in terms of what they do.

The definition of identity includes both—what we do with our time and how we feel about the use we make of it. It is the unity and integration of all aspects of self, including conscious and unconscious perceptions.

The formation of identity, according to the neo-Freudian Erik Erikson, is largely an unconscious process, except when inner conditions and outer circumstances are discordant, and the individual becomes out of sync with his or her true identity.

Some people find that their chosen life's work does not resonate with their true being. Consider the talented Mr. Ripley, who hates his work as a men's room attendant in a symphony hall. When the auditorium has been vacated after the concert one night, he sits at the piano and plays Bach's *Italian Concerto*, quite movingly. Being a musician, however, is just one of the many facets of his multifaceted personality and, as we shall see, he ardently admires a man whose identity has coalesced and who he imagines has put his life together.

If identity encompasses the complexity of "who I am," then its formation requires integrating and shaping discrete facets of the self into a unique being. When this fails to occur, mortification occurs. Young man Thoreau had an "as-if" personality, and he was mortified when many who knew him considered that he borrowed his identity from his older mentor, Ralph Waldo Emerson. Thoreau biographer Walter Harding writes:

> It was a bugbear Thoreau had to live with . . . to stand in the shadow of Emerson and have his most independent writings and actions dismissed as "Emersonian."[1]

THE "AS-IF" PERSONALITY AND THE SEARCH FOR A SENSE OF SELF

In those with an "as-if" personality, the psychoanalyst Helene Deutsche writes, "the individual's whole relationship to life has something about it which is lacking in genuineness and yet outwardly runs 'as if' it were complete."[2]

These persons may be gifted and intelligent, but their artistic or intellectual productions lack originality. Chiefly, they are imitative in their relationships with other people in a chameleonic way, adopting the others' ways of walking, talking, or dress. Although the relationship may begin well, problems invariably arise. Deutsch writes:

> At first the love, friendship, and attachment of an "as if" person have something very rewarding for the partner. If it is a woman, she seems to be the quintessence of feminine devotion, an impression which is particularly imparted by her passivity and readiness for identification. Soon, however, the lack of real warmth brings such an emptiness and dullness to the emotional atmosphere that the man as a rule precipitously breaks off the relationship. . . . At the first opportunity the former object is exchanged for a new one and the process is repeated.[3]

The same emptiness and lack of originality appear in the moral judgments of these people. Literally unprincipled, their morals and ideals are the reflections of those of other persons, good or bad:

> Attaching themselves with great ease to social, ethical, and religious groups, they seek, by adhering to a group, to give content and reality to their inner emptiness and establish the banality of their existence by identification. Overenthusiastic adherence to one philosophy can be quickly and completely replaced by another contradictory one without the slightest trace of inward transformation—simply as a result of some accidental regrouping of the circle of acquaintances or the like.[4]

Olenka Plemmyannikova in Chekhov's "The Darling", Woody Allen's character Zelig, Patricia Highsmith's talented Tom Ripley, Frank Abagnale (author of the autobiography *Catch Me If You Can*), and young man Thoreau all had problems crystallizing an authentic sense of self. Each dealt with the mortifying shame that manifested in different ways, as we shall see.

NOTES

1. Walter Harding, *The Days of Henry Thoreau* (New York: Dover, 1992), 65.

2. Helene Deutsch, "Some Forms of Emotional Disturbance and Their Relationship to Schizophrenia" [1942], *Neuroses and Character Types: Clinical Psychological Studies* (New York, International Universities Press, 1965), 262, 263.

3. Ibid., 265.

4. Ibid., 266.

Chapter Two

Anton Chekhov's "The Darling": Imitative Pseudo-Relationships

Anton Chekhov (1860–1904) achieves greatness as a short-story writer partly through psychological minimalism. Little may actually occur in the course of many of his tales, but much is revealed through apparently insignificant details. In "The Darling," for example, Olenka's flaw, an imitative modus vivendi, becomes increasingly apparent in the course of three marriages, which fail despite her "charm."

By combining the physician's nonjudgmental, observing eye with the compassion of a great artist, Chekhov allows his characters to exhibit identifiable psychiatric syndromes. "The Darling" offers a remarkable example of Helene Deutsch's "as-if" personality type. Deutsch could have been describing Olenka when she wrote:

> Any object will do as a bridge for identification. . . . In spite of the adhesiveness which the "as if" person brings to every relationship, when he is . . . abandoned he displays either a rush of affective reactions which are "as if" and thus spurious, or a frank absence of affectivity. At the very first opportunity the former object is exchanged for a new one and the process is repeated.[1]

FOUR IMITATIVE "LOVES"

In the relationships with her three husbands and with the son of the third, Olenka adopts the identity of her partners—first a theater manager, then a lumber merchant, and finally a veterinarian. The last "love" of her life is the veterinarian's young son.

Early in the story Chekhov makes explicit part of her problem, evident from her earliest childhood years:

She was always enamored of someone and could not live otherwise. At first it had been her papa, who was now ill and sat in an armchair in a darkened room, breathing with difficulty. Then she had devoted her affections to her aunt, who used to come from Bryansk every other year. Still earlier, when she went to school, she had been in love with her French teacher.[2]

Soon after meeting the theater manager, Kukin, the narrator relates that

what Kukin said about artists and the theater she would repeat. Like him she despised the public for its ignorance and indifference to art; she took a hand in the rehearsals, correcting the actors, kept an eye on the musicians, and when there was an unfavorable notice in the local paper, she wept and went to see the editor about it.[3]

Olenka thrives in the marriage, gains weight, and beams with happiness, but matters do not go well with her husband, who becomes sallow, grows thinner, and complains of financial losses, although attendance at the theater is fairly good considering it is wintertime.

Eventually Kukin dies and Olenka, hearing the news, sobs: "Vanitchka, my precious, my sweet! Why did we ever meet! . . . To whom can your poor unhappy Olenka turn?"[4]

Three months later, however, returning from mass in deep mourning, she meets Pustovalov, the manager of a lumber yard, who walks her back home from church to her gate. Olenka is transformed: "All the rest of the day she heard his sedate voice, and as soon as she closed her eyes she had a vision of his dark beard." Three days later Pustovalov drops by for a ten-minute visit and says very little, "but Olenka fell in love with him, so deeply that she stayed awake all night burning as with fever. . . . The match was soon arranged and then came the wedding."[5]

Before long, Olenka gets involved with her husband's lumber business and feels as though she has been dealing in lumber for years:

It seemed to her that she had been in the lumber business for ages, that lumber was the most important, the most essential thing in the world; and she found something intimate and touching in the very sound of such words as "beam, log, batten, plank, box board, lath, scantling, slab. . . ."[6]

Deutsch notes that those with the "as-if" personality possess "a passive attitude to the environment with a highly plastic readiness to pick up signals from the outer world and to mold oneself and one's behavior accordingly."[7] Thus, Olenka becomes as involved in the lumber business as she was in the theater. Whatever ideas her husband has, she adopts as her own. If he thinks that the room is hot or that business is slow, she thinks so too. If her husband does not care for being entertained and stays home on holidays, she does the same.

When Olenka's friends suggest she should go to the circus or the theater and spend less time at home she replies, "Vasichka and I have no time for the theatre. We are working people, we're not interested in such foolishness. What good are these theatres?"[8] She says this even though, a few months before, she had remarked that "the theater was the most remarkable, the most important, and the most essential thing in the world, and that it was only the theater that could give true pleasure and make you a cultivated and humane person."

One is reminded of Deutsch's comments about how "quickly and completely" the "as-if" individual replaces one philosophy of life with a different, even contradictory, one, "simply as a result of some accidental regrouping of the circle of acquaintances or the like."

Unfortunately, Pustovalov dies and once again Olenka is widowed. "To whom shall I turn now, my darling?" she sobs at the burial. "How can I live without you, wretched and unhappy as I am? Pity me, good people, left alone in the world."[9]

True to form, she is able to replace him, and within six months neighbors observe Olenka doffing the widow's weeds and opening the shutters. She has met Smirnin, the veterinarian who is renting a wing in the Pustovalov house.

Soon, upon meeting an acquaintance, Olenka complains about the lack of veterinary inspection in the town—the reason there is so much illness around. Indeed, she insists that "the health of domestic animals must be as well cared for as the health of human beings." According to Chekhov's narrator, "She now repeated the veterinary's words and held the same opinion about everything that he did."[10]

The psychoanalyst Annie Reich noted that those with the imitative propensity are not particularly finicky in their selections:

> The women of the "as-if" type show a lack of discrimination in the choice of objects. Some of them can glorify anything and are ready to identify themselves with anyone happening to enter their sphere of life. In the case of others, their admiration is tied to one condition: the man's worth must be recognized by other people. The content of his qualities is irrelevant.[11]

After a while, Olenka's emptiness and need to cling become troublesome to Smirnin. When he has visitors, regimental colleagues, Olenka, who pours tea or serves supper, always begins to talk of cattle plague, pearl disease, or the municipal slaughter-houses. Smirnin becomes terribly embarrassed and when the guests depart, he grasps her by the arms and hisses angrily. When veterinarians speak among themselves, he insists, she should not butt in.[12] She turns to him, amazed and alarmed, asking him what she *should* talk about. Discussing the "as-if" woman, Reich notes: "They take over the man's personality, interests and values completely; it is as if they had no judgment of their own, no ego of their own."[13]

When Smirnin's regiment relocates, Olenka's great emptiness once again surfaces: "She looked apathetically at the empty courtyard, thought of nothing, and later, when night came, she would go to bed and dream of the empty courtyard."[14] She is incapable of performing even the most rudimentary thought processes:

> Above all, and worst of all, she no longer had any opinions whatever. She saw objects about her and understood what was going on, but she could not form an opinion about anything and did not know what to talk about. And how terrible it is not to have any opinions! You see, for instance, a bottle, or the rain, or a peasant driving in a cart, but what is the bottle for, or the rain, or the peasant, what is the meaning of them, you can't tell, and you couldn't, even if they paid you a thousand rubles.[15]

When she was with Kukin or Pustovalov or the veterinary surgeon, Olenka could explain everything and give her opinion about anything they talked about, "But now there was the same emptiness in her head and in her heart as in her courtyard."[16]

Smirnin, whose regiment has now returned, appears one day with his wife and ten-year-old son, Sasha. Olenka invites them to move in with her and when they do she begins to feel like her old self again: "The old smile had come back to her face, and she was lively and spry, as though she had waked from a long sleep."[17]

Olenka's relentless search for a human attachment began in childhood, with the absence of parents. In "The Darling," her mother is never mentioned and her father is referred to twice. The first time he is ill, seated in an armchair in a darkened room, breathing with difficulty. Later in the story we are told that the father died long ago and that his armchair is in the attic, covered with dust and missing a leg.

Olenka's perception of her father as defective invites comparison with a case Deutsch reports in which there is a relative absence of the father, who was in and out of hospitals. The patient

> tried to explain, as something very fascinating and wonderful, his absences as he was moved to and from a sanitarium and an isolated room at home, always under nursing care. Thus she built a myth around her father, replacing him in

fantasy by a mysterious man. . . . It seems that a disappointment shattered the strong relationship with the mother, that the mysterious absence of the father made it impossible for the little girl to find in him a substitute when her relationship to her mother was shaken, and that further relationships to objects [family members] remained at the stage of identification.[18]

With an absent mother and a defective father, Olenka is fated to search for someone to fill the void. When the men in her life (who have been little more than space-occupying masses) vanish, Olenka's vast emptiness returns and her cognitive functioning becomes impaired.

Olenka has a nightmare during the time that she is married to Pustovalov, which symbolizes the nightmare of her life:

At night she would dream of whole mountains of boards and planks, of endless caravans of carts hauling lumber out of town to distant points. She would dream that a regiment of beams, 28 feet by 8 inches, standing on end, was marching in the lumberyard, that beams, logs, and slabs were crashing against each other with the hollow sound of dry wood, that they kept tumbling down and rising again, piling themselves on each other. Olenka would scream in her sleep.[19]

These boards, planks, beams, logs, and slabs could symbolize the caravan of suitors in her life. They crash against each other, tumble down, rise up, and pile on each other in nightmarish fashion.

A "RUSSIAN MAUPASSANT"

Because of his supremacy as a short-story writer, Chekhov has been called "the Russian Maupassant." There are similarities between the two great writers, but Leonard Woolf drew a distinction many years ago:

Whereas Maupassant's mental atmosphere is clear, keen and strong, with a touch of a hard cold wind, Chekhov's is born of a softer, warmer, kindlier earth. Had Maupassant written "The Darling," he would have been less patient with Olenka's lack of brains, more cynical over her forgetfulness of her first and second husbands. And a French Olenka would, in fact, have been less naïve than the Russian woman, and in that respect more open to criticism.[20]

Careful readers of Chekhov will note, however, that Olenka is neither brainless nor forgetful but has a subtle personality disorder revealed in mimicked, unfulfilled relationships. Woolf also misses the point in his comparisons:

Chekhov spends his time drawing the shallow woman. . . . Nor are Chekhov's men and women even interesting in their abnormality. He has no figures like Turgenev's Rudin and Levretsky, Dostoyevsky's Raskolnikov and Dmitry Karamazov, our affection for whom, despite their weakness or sinfulness, outlast our memory of what happens to them.[1]

Although Olenka has her problems, she is neither shallow nor lacking in interest. And we by no means forget the memory of this "quiet, kind, softhearted girl, with meek, gentle eyes and . . . very good health."

Having contributed to the demise of two husbands, the departure of a third, and blurred the boundaries of her relationship with an adolescent boy, Olenka's "full pink cheeks, her soft white neck with a dark birthmark on it, and the kind, artless smile that came into her face when she listened to anything pleasant," reverberate when her "as-if" imitative mode comes to mind.

It is as if Woolf had compared a Schubert "Impromptu" to Bach's "Art of the Fugue." The impromptu is deceptively simple, as is Chekhov's sketch. Both have a sketchy appearance, unlike the masterpieces, but neither Schubert nor Chekhov can be accused of ignoring uncommon and important complex phenomena.

NOTES

1. Deutsch, 265.

2. Anton Chekhov, *The Portable Chekhov*, Avram Yarmolinsky, ed. and tr. (New York, Penguin, 1988), 397.

3. Ibid., 399.

4. Ibid., 400.

5. Ibid., 401.

6. Ibid., 402.

7. Deutsch, 265.

8. *Portable Chekhov*, 402.

9. Ibid., 404.

10. Ibid., 405.

11. Annie Reich, "Narcissistic Object Choice in Women," *Psychoanalytic Contributions* (New York: International Universities Press, 1953), 193.

12. *Portable Chekhov*, 405.

13. Reich 191.

14. *Portable Chekhov*, 406.

15. Ibid.

16. The title of Deutsch's essay comes to mind: "Some forms of emotional illness and their relationship to schizophrenia."

17. *Portable Chekhov*, 408.

18. Deutsch, 271–72.

19. *Portable Chekhov*, 402.

20. Quoted in Anton Chekhov, *Ward No. 6 and Other Stories*, David Plante, ed. (New York: Barnes and Noble, 2003), 362.

21. Ibid., 365.

Chapter Three

Woody Allen's *Zelig*:
The Human Chameleon

In this fake documentary (or "mockumentary") Woody Allen plays the part of Leonard Zelig, a man afflicted with a baffling psychiatric disorder.

Using lenses, cameras, photo stills, and sound equipment of the 1930s, *Zelig* has the veracity of a documentary film of that era. The film's vintage footage includes cameo appearances by Adolf Hitler, Charles Lindbergh, Al Capone, William Randolph Hearst, Josephine Baker, Lou Gehrig, Hermann Goering, and F. Scott Fitzgerald, who first spots Zelig at a party.

In the course of his encounters with persons in his milieu who are important to him, Zelig immediately assumes their physical and mental identity.

When this human chameleon lives in Chinatown, for example, he instantly develops Asian facial features and begins speaking in Chinese. In the presence of obese men, he becomes extremely fat. In a mental hospital, he takes on the identity of a psychiatrist, and says, "I worked with Freud in Vienna. We broke over the concept of penis envy—Freud felt it should be limited to girls." *Zelig*, although fake, tells the truth (albeit in exaggerated fashion) about the "as-if" personality described by the psychoanalyst Helene Deutsch in 1942.

Allen based his screenplay on Deutsch's essay "Some forms of Emotional Disturbance and Their Relationship to Schizophrenia," which is reflected in the working title of his movie, *Identity Crisis and Its Relationship to Personality Disorder.*[1] Persons with this disorder, Deutsch observed, unconsciously imitate the thought, affect, and behavior of others, as a substitute for their lack of a sense of self.

Zelig, who winds up in a Manhattan hospital cared for by Dr. Eudora Fletcher (Mia Farrow), a psychiatrist, was bullied in his life by anti-Semites. His parents, who never took his part, blamed him for everything and sided with the anti-Semites. Having no protection against bullies, he adopted a lifestyle based on the motto, "If you can't beat 'em, join 'em."

From a psychoanalytic perspective it would appear that without a sense of identity Leonard Zelig's self disappears. Having no sense of self, he can easily adopt the identity of others, becoming like them—Pope Pius on the Vatican balcony during Easter week; or Hitler ranting at a gathering in Nuremberg.

In Yiddish *zelig* means "blessed," yet beneath the film's comic exterior, Zelig is the opposite of blessed: he suffers from the absence of meaningful relationships and a lack of identity. In the end, however, after treatment with Dr. Fletcher, whom he loves and marries, we learn from the voice-over narrative that "it was, after all, not the approbation of many but the love of one woman that changed his life. . . . Zelig's episodes of character change grew less and less frequent and eventually his malady disappeared completely."[2]

NOTES

1. Given by the Internet Movie Database, among other sources (http://www.imdb.com/title/tt0086637/—Accessed 9/24/2006).

2. Woody Allen, *Three Films of Woody Allen: "Zelig," "Broadway Danny Rose," "The Purple Rose of Cairo"* (London: Faber & Faber, 1990), 129.

Chapter Four

Patricia Highsmith's *The Talented Mr. Ripley*: Better a Fake Somebody than a Real Nobody

"I always thought it would be better to be a fake somebody than a real nobody," says Tom Ripley, the talented underachiever of Patricia Highsmith's (1921–1995) novel *The Talented Mr. Ripley*, which was adapted into a popular film in 1999 by Anthony Minghella. This precept also guided the practices of Frank Abagnale, Jr., as narrated in his autobiography *Catch Me If You Can*, also made into a motion picture, discussed further below.

Helene Deutsch's concept of the "as-if" personality applies to both Ripley and to his nonfictional counterpart, Abagnale. Neither Ripley nor Abagnale had an authentic sense of self, and both adopted identities of those whom they admired, their ego ideal.

The possibility of reinventing the self, as Ripley and Abagnale both did, is a longstanding American practice, as Michiko Kakutani perceptively writes in the *New York Times*.[1] It was brought over by colonists who left Europe to begin afresh in the New World, and is seen again in F. Scott Fitzgerald's character Jay Gatsby, who tries to inhabit his platonic conception of himself. Describing the proclivity of Americans to remake their lives, Kakutani writes of their "moving West with the frontier to start over, or moving East to the big city to erase their provincial roots, shucking off familial legacies and changing their names, their looks, their histories."

From this perspective, Tom Ripley is a prototypically American arriviste. When the man he idealizes, Dickie Greenleaf, Princeton '53, asks Tom what he does for a living, since he has not crystallized a vocational identity, his self-reinventions are many and varied:

> I can do a number of things. Valeting, babysitting, accounting. . . . I can forge a signature, fly a helicopter, handle dice, impersonate practically anybody,

cook—and do a one-man show in a nightclub in case the regular entertainer's sick.[2]

Multitalented Tom Ripley can do almost anything and imitate almost anybody because his sense of self, practically nonexistent, does not intrude. The only talent he lacks is one which lies buried within—the talent to be himself.

We first meet the movie version of Ripley in the men's room of a symphony hall, where he works as an attendant, brushing dandruff off the Brooks Brothers suits of the well-to-do, picking up tips. He detests the work and is ashamed of himself.

In the following scene, Ripley is on the floor above the toilets, seated at the piano on the concert stage, playing Bach's *Italian Concerto* to an empty concert auditorium. In his element, beneath the cloak of shame—wearing spectacles like Clark Kent—we glimpse his Superman pride. Then the stage manager, closing the house, makes a few disparaging remarks to the young man at the keyboard and shuts off the lights, leaving Ripley in the dark.

Ripley is invited to play the piano at a social function in the suburbs, but does not have a jacket to wear for the occasion. He borrows a blazer on which the Princeton logo is emblazoned, and Herbert Greenleaf, a ship-building magnate, mistakes him for a friend of his son, Dickie Greenleaf, Jr., '53. From then on, Tom insinuates himself into the world of those on whom he waited in the men's lavatory.

Greenleaf offers Tom the job of coaxing his son, living the life of a millionaire playboy in Mongibello, to leave the Amalfi coast and return to the United States. Ripley accepts the assignment, and soon finds himself overseas with the bronzed, apparently self-assured Dickie, who has a trust fund, a seaside apartment with maid service, a girlfriend, and, to ride her around, a Vespa motor scooter. Tom falls in love with the image of the man. In reality, Dickie is estranged from his parents, is unable to make a commitment to his girlfriend (with whom he has no sex), is a dabbler at art, and has a streak of violence, which surfaced at Princeton.

Tom offers Dickie friendship, admiration, and a hero-worshiper's love, but cannot convince his idol to return to the United States, despite his best efforts.

Taking a walk on the beach with Dickie, they encounter a group of young male sunbather-athletes constructing a human pyramid. When a swarthy young man of seventeen is boosted to the top, Tom shouts "Bravo," but Dickie makes a homophobic remark about Cannes being full of "queers." Highsmith writes:

It startled Tom, then he felt that sharp thrust of shame, the same shame he had felt in Mongibello when Dickie had said, *Marge thinks you are* [queer]. All right, Tom thought, the acrobats were fairies. Maybe Cannes was full of fairies. So what? Tom's fists were clenched tight in his trouser pockets. He remembered Aunt Dottie's taunt: *Sissy! He's a sissy from the ground up. Just like his father!*[3]

Tom feels mortified. Once more he is a failure. He has been unable to influence Dickie to return to the United States, though he has given him his love and admiration, and feels he's a sissy like his father—possibly also "queer." Murderous impulses arise:

A crazy emotion of hate, of affection, of impatience and frustration was swelling in him, hampering his breathing. He wanted to kill Dickie. It . . . left him with a feeling of shame.[4]

Ripley murders Greenleaf and assumes his identity: It felt "wonderful to sit in a famous café and think of tomorrow and tomorrow being Dickie Greenleaf." After police investigators make it dangerous for Tom continue in the guise of the object of his affections, he detests the idea of reclaiming his former identity:

He hated becoming Tom Ripley again, hated being nobody, hated putting on his old set of habits again, and feeling that people looked down on him and were bored with him unless he put on an act for them like a clown, feeling incompetent and incapable of doing anything with himself except entertaining people for minutes at a time.[5]

THE PARABLE OF THE TALENTS

Talented Tom Ripley calls to mind another talented person, the servant in Matthew 25:14–30 who also buries his talent. The story recounts how the master of the servants, who is preparing to travel afar, gives each servant talents (a natural ability/an ancient monetary unit): five to one, two to another, and one to the last.

When he returns, he tells each of the two servants who have used their talents productively, "Well done, thou good and faithful servant: thou hast been faithful over a few things, I will make thee ruler over many things." But to the servant who had buried his talent the master wrathfully exclaims:

Take therefore the talent from him, and give it unto him which hath ten talents. For unto every one that hath shall be given . . . but from him that hath not shall be taken away even that which he hath.

The New Testament master casts that servant into the dark, just as the stage manager of the concert hall shuts off the lights on Ripley, who sits alone in the darkness pondering his buried talent—the courage to be himself. Being himself, he said, felt as if he was putting on "a grease-spotted unpressed suit of clothes," so unlike the dapper Brooks Brothers, gray-flannel suits from which he brushed dandruff in his former job as a men's room attendant, a humiliating livelihood.

Ripley is highly motivated to dream up scenarios to avoid being himself and, as Highsmith writes, "His stories are good because he imagined them intensely, so intensely that he came to believe them."

Both Joseph Conrad's protagonist Lord Jim (as we shall see) and Highsmith's Tom Ripley bury the talent to be themselves, which leads to further bloodshed. In Jim's case it is followed by a murder (really a manipulated suicide); in Tom's, to serial homicides.

NOTES

1. Michiko Kakutani, "A Radical on the Run, Determined to Escape the Past," *New York Times*, Feb. 3, 2006.

2. Patricia Highsmith, *The Talented Mr. Ripley* (New York: Random House / Vintage, 1992), 58.

3. Ibid., 98–99.

4. Ibid., 100.

5. Ibid., 192. Deutsch compares the "as if" life to "the performance of an actor who is technically well trained but who lacks the necessary spark to make his impersonations true to life" (Deutsch 264). It should be noted that although Deutsch's "as if" phenomenon differs from that of depersonalization—in which the individual himself is conscious of feeling empty and complains of it—Deutsch broadens the "as if" category to include certain cases in which the patient, rather like Tom Ripley, does complain of lack of feeling (ibid., 263, 273, 275–76).

Chapter Five

Reinvented Selves: Frank Abagnale's *Catch Me If You Can* and James Thurber's "The Secret Life of Walter Mitty"

The autobiography by Frank Abagnale, Jr. (1948–), *Catch Me If You Can*, adapted into a motion picture by Steven Spielberg, depicts his half-dozen teenage years as a con man who steals over $2.5 million through forgery and fraud until he is apprehended by the FBI.

The precipitating event for Abagnale seems to have occurred at the age of sixteen, when his mother divorced his father, a once-prosperous businessman reduced to a post-office job, and Frank had to decide with whom he wanted to live. He chose his father, but soon dropped out of high school, ran away from home, and began forging checks to support himself. Ashamed of a lack of identity, he began impersonating people whose vocational identity he admired, and became a master of deception.

By his twenty-first birthday, he had masqueraded as a Pan American pilot for two years, obtaining a pilot's uniform from a supply company by pretending he had lost his own. He made a counterfeit Pan Am ID card from a stationer's sample model, and obtained an FAA license by resizing a display plaque.

Subsequently, he impersonated a pediatrician in a Georgia hospital for eleven months, then forged a Harvard University Law School diploma, passed the bar exam in Louisiana, and obtained work at the office of the state attorney general. He forged a transcript claiming a Ph.D. from Columbia University and taught sociology for a summer term at a university in Utah.

Apart from the teaching stint, it should be noted, Abagnale never put his purported professional skills into practice. For example, he did not know how to fly a plane, but used the glamour and authority of the uniform to travel widely, defrauding financial institutions across the United States.

An imposter for over five years, Abagnale worked under eight identities, and passed bad checks worth several million dollars in every state and twenty-six foreign countries. As to his motive for forging checks, defrauding banks, and dressing handsomely, all he wanted, he states, was to make his father feel proud of him (which, alas, he was never able to do).[1]

Abagnale's impersonations were important because they removed him from the person it pained him to be (like Ripley) and positioned him in the role of a socially admired citizen. They brought him instant respect, which he never received at home, possibly because of the parents' marital disharmonies. He explains:

> There is enchantment in a uniform, especially one that marks the wearer as a person of some skill, courage or achievement. . . . Men looked at me admiringly, or enviously. Pretty women and girls smiled at me. Airport policemen nodded courteously. Pilots and stewardesses smiled, spoke to me or lifted a hand in greeting as they passed. Every man, woman and child who noticed me seemed warm and friendly.[2]

Like his fictional counterpart Tom Ripley, Frank Abagnale found it "better to be a fake somebody than a real nobody." Both chose identities that were uplifting to them. Abagnale writes: "Whenever I felt lonely, depressed, rejected or doubtful of my own worth, the uniform brought me dignity and respect. Without it on, at times, I felt useless and dejected."[3]

In an unlikely place for a transformative revelation—working as a projectionist for a movie theater—Abagnale had an insight into the talent that he had buried during his spree:

> I was making good money, but I was there five nights a week. Caged in a small room with nothing to do, really, save to watch the same movie over and over again. I thought to myself that I was smarter than that, that I was ignoring and wasting real talents that I possessed.[4]

After serving a prison stint, Abagnale unburied his talent over the next quarter of a century, while working in the Financial Crimes Unit of the Federal Bureau of Investigation, sleuthing identity theft. Since his own identity was once stolen by his low self-esteem, he currently watches over it scrupulously: "The Frank Abagnale I was was an egotistical, unethical, unscrupulous criminal," he reportedly has said. "The Frank Abagnale I am today is a good father and a good husband."

Having founded Abagnale & Associates, which advises the business world about fraud prevention, Abagnale once again became a multimillionaire, but this time through his consulting services.[5] He also has made over

twenty million dollars from the sale of his three books: *Catch Me If You Can,*
The Art of the Steal, and *Real U Guide to Identity Theft.* He is outspokenly
proud of his accomplishments in the world of law and order: "Modesty is
not one of my virtues." But this is an improvement over the way things were
when, as he puts it, "Virtue was not one of my virtues."

THURBER'S WALTER MITTY,
"THE OLD MAN [WHO] AIN'T AFRAID OF HELL"

James Thurber's (1894–1961) "The Secret Life of Walter Mitty" (1939) is a
fictional account of a henpecked, middle-class, outwardly conventional man
who escapes a monotonous life with frequent daydreams of glory. In one fantasy he is the tough and fearless commander of a huge, eight-engined Navy
hydroplane hurtling through a hurricane, the worst storm in twenty years,
who has the respect of his crew: "The Old Man'll get us through. . . . The Old
Man ain't afraid of hell," the crewmen say to one another.[6]

"Not so fast! . . . You're driving too fast! What are you driving so fast
for?" exclaims Mrs. Mitty. "You know I don't like to go more than forty."
She has disrupted her husband's fantasies, and the pounding of the cylinders
of the Commander's SN202, "*ta-pocketa-pocketa-pocketa-pocketa-pocketa,*"
decreases.[7]

Mitty, like Olenka Plemmyannikova, Leonard Zelig, Frank Abagnale, Tom
Ripley, and Henry Thoreau (to whom we turn next) would rather be someone admirable—not himself. Olenka, Zelig, Mitty, and Thoreau assume the
identities of others unconsciously, whereas Abagnale and Ripley are quite
conscious of being impostors, although unaware of the reason they find their
authentic selves repulsive. Becoming effective is an important prerequisite
for self-acceptance, and the next section presents a real-life equivalent to the
otherworldly Olenka.

NOTES

1. Abagnale, Frank W., Jr., with Stan Redding, *Catch Me if You Can* (New York:
Grosset & Dunlap, 1980), 5.

2. Ibid., 40.

3. Ibid., 41.

4. Ibid., 251.

5. Quite perceptively, Abagnale concludes his autobiography with this observation: "Actually, I haven't changed. All the needs that made me a criminal are still

there. I have simply found a legal and socially acceptable way to fulfill those needs. I'm still a con artist. I'm just putting down a positive con these days, as opposed to the negative con I used in the past. I have simply redirected the talents I've always possessed" (ibid., 253).

6. James Thurber, *The Secret Lives of Walter Mitty and of James Thurber* (New York: Harper Collins, 2006), n.p. [1].

7. Ibid.

Chapter Six

Henry David Thoreau's Alter Egos: Ralph Waldo Emerson and John Thoreau, Jr.

The two most important people in the life of the philosopher Henry David Thoreau (1817–1862) were his brother, John Thoreau, Jr., and his mentor, Ralph Waldo Emerson. His relationship with both of them was characterized by "as-if" mimicry.

The two major events in Thoreau's life—living in the pond-side cabin at Walden and going to jail rather than pay taxes—were significant for several reasons. Above all, they led to the writing of *Walden* and "Civil Disobedience."

These two events also played a major part in Thoreau's development of a sense of self. Living at Walden provided feelings of autonomy, and going to jail helped Thoreau to divest himself of his imitative attachment to Emerson.

In contrast, Thoreau remained symbiotically attached to his beloved older brother, as we shall see, even after John's tragic early death from lockjaw.

MIRRORING RALPH WALDO EMERSON

Thoreau's father, a retiring type of person who was overshadowed by his outspoken wife, never really appreciated their unusual son. Ralph Waldo Emerson, fifteen years Thoreau's senior, was the father that Thoreau never had.

Emerson was the first great man in Thoreau's life, and Henry was profoundly affected by their encounter. From the time they first met in 1837 until Thoreau's death in 1862, the two saw each other frequently, often daily, even after the decline in the intensity of their friendship that began in 1846, the year of Thoreau's civil disobedience. When Emerson traveled abroad, he arranged for his protégé to live at his home and look after his grounds and family.

Emerson, one of America's first intellectual celebrities, had a wide circle of friends; a gracious, sympathetic wife; a fine Concord home; a well-stocked library; and a charismatic presence. He went out of his way to be informative to the "erect" (Emerson's word) youth, lent him books, introduced him to guest visitors, and started Thoreau on his most extensive literary venture—his three-million-word, lifelong journal.

Thoreau's unconscious imitation of Emerson was so evident that first-time visitors and old friends alike noted similarities of voice, gesture, way of walking, hair style, handwriting, etc. A fellow Harvard graduate, David Green Haskins, who was so familiar with his colleague's voice that he "could have recognized him by it in the dark," found it showed no resemblance to Emerson's voice before they met. Afterward, he said that with his eyes closed he could not determine which of the two was speaking, and called it "a notable instance of unconscious imitation."[1]

The author Ednah Littlehale Cheney observed that Thoreau was "all overlaid by an imitation of Emerson; talks like him, puts out his arm like him, brushes his hair in the same way, etc."[2] Franklin B. Sanborn, who boarded with the Thoreau family upon settling in Concord in 1855 and knew Henry thereafter, saw in him "a pocket edition of Mr. Emerson, as far as outward appearance goes. . . .He talks like Mr. Emerson and so spoils the good things which he says; for what in Mr. Emerson is charming, becomes ludicrous in Thoreau, because an imitation."[3]

Ellery Channing, a close companion, emphasized the unconscious nature of the mimicry: "In Emerson's mode of writing from his Journals, Thoreau imitated him; and yet there was no such thing as conscious imitation in him. His handwriting, too, has such a resemblance to Emerson's that I could hardly tell them apart. It was very strange for Henry never imitated anybody."[4]

"THE ARM OF AN ELM"

Although those with an "as-if" personality give the impression of complete normalcy and, according to Helene Deutsch, are often creatively gifted, bringing a clear understanding to intellectual matters, they exclude feelings from their interpersonal contacts.

Many have commented on Thoreau's aloofness. Emerson, for instance, wrote that taking his arm was like "taking up the arm of an elm."[5] George W. Curtis, the editor, noted that Thoreau never lounged or slouched, and that he used "a staccato style of speech, every word coming separately and distinctly, as if preserving the same cool isolation in the sentence as [he] did in society."[6]

Thoreau's emotional distance is evident in the description of him by Harrison Blake, a devoted friend and correspondent:

> Our relation, as I look back on it, seems almost an impersonal one, and illustrates well his remark that "our thoughts are the epochs in our lives: all else is but as a journal of the winds that blew while we were here." When together, we had little inclination to talk of personal matters. His aim was directed so steadily and earnestly towards what is essential in our experience, that beyond all others of whom I have known, he made but a single impression on me. Geniality, versatility, personal familiarity are, of course, agreeable in those about us, and seem necessary in human intercourse, but I did not miss them in Thoreau, who was . . . such an effectual witness to what is highest and most precious in life.[7]

Going to jail, even for one day, in 1846, rather that paying taxes to support a war he considered unjust—acting from principle—was the entering wedge that enabled him to separate from Emerson, who considered Thoreau's act "mean and skulking and in bad taste . . . the prison is one step to suicide."[8]

Finally, in 1851, Thoreau articulated the problem he had with his mentor, a lack of trust: "Ah, I yearn toward thee, my friend, but I have no confidence in thee; . . . I am not thou; thou art not I."[9] Thoreau, at long last, was able to be his own man and could finally answer the question he had posed at the age of twenty-three, seven years after meeting Emerson: "If I am not I who will be?"[10]

MIRRORING JOHN THOREAU, JR.

John Thoreau, Jr., was a genial, charming, and gregarious person who was also at one with nature. Henry imitated his ways of relating to field and stream (but not those of relating to people, evidently). There was much opportunity for emulation, since they spent a great deal of time together, especially out of doors, and attended the same public school in Concord, Massachusetts.

The boys' father, described as "a mousey sort of man,"[11] related to his unusual sons with tolerance, but unenthusiastically. John was not only a devoted brother, but filled in for the homebound father the way Thoreau's other father surrogate, Emerson, rarely did. Henry learned from John how to recognize birds by their calls, trees by their leaves; where to find Indian arrowheads; and especially how to pay close attention to the progress of the seasons beneath the arrowy pines.

Henry's "as-if" mimicry of John is apparent in the simple, natural lifestyle that corresponded with his older brother's, but also in the unconscious mimicry of his older brother's moribund state when John was dying of lockjaw in January 1842. Lidian (Mrs. Ralph Waldo) Emerson, who knew the Thoreau brothers well, wrote:

> After J. had taken leave of all the family he said to Henry now sit down and talk to me of Nature and Poetry, I shall be a good listener for it is difficult for me to interrupt you. During the hour in which he died, he looked at Henry with a "transcendent smile full of Heaven" (I think this was H.'s expression) and Henry "found himself returning it" and this was the last communication that passed between them.[12]

The smile was not one of bliss but the *risus sardonicus,* the "sardonic grin" caused by the deadly contractions of the powerful muscles of mastication in tetanus. Henry's guilt-aggravated facsimile lockjaw, a conversion disorder which he contracted a few days after John's death, resulted from a profound identification with and unconscious imitation of that macabre smile.

Henry so idolized his brother that he continued John's life for him after his death. Consider the eulogy read at John's funeral by Barzillai Frost, minister of the First Parish Church in Concord. As Thoreau biographer Walter Harding noted, it "could have just as appropriately been read for Henry Thoreau twenty years later," so thoroughly had Henry assimilated his brother's life style:

> He had a love of nature, even from childhood amounting to enthusiasm. He spent many of his leisure hours in straying over these hills and along the banks of the streams. There is not a hill, nor a tree, nor a bird, nor a flower of marked beauty in all this neighborhood that he was not familiar with, and any new bird or flower he discovered gave him the most unfeigned delight, and he would dwell with it and seem to commune with it for hours. He spent also many a serene and loving evening gazing upon the still moonlight scene and the blazing aurora, or looking into the bright firmament, radiant with the glory of God. . . .
>
> The benevolence of the deceased appeared in his love of animals, in the pleasure he took in making children happy, and in his readiness to give up his time to oblige all. He had a heart to feel and a voice to speak for all classes of suffering humanity; and the cause of the poor inebriate, the slave, the ignorant and depraved, was very dear to him. . . .
>
> Of his religious opinions I must speak with less confidence. He has been affected no doubt by the revolutionary opinions abroad in society in regard to inspiration and religious instructions, as it is very natural the young should. But there has been a tendency of late in his mind, I have thought, to those views which have fortified the minds of the great majority of the wise and good in all ages. (I may be mistaken in supposing that he adopted the transcendental views to any considerable extent.) But, however his theories *about* religion were unsettled, his principles and religious feelings were always unshaken. The religious sentiment had been awakened, and he manifested it in his tastes, feelings and conversation.[13]

The eulogy, as is often the case, overflows with benignity and lumps together several social-reform causes of the time. Not every trait ascribed to John, if true, was imitated by Henry. In particular, in spite of his fervent abolitionist beliefs, Thoreau never joined any organization in support of the "cause of the slave." And in his daily life, the high-minded moralist showed little tolerance for the inebriate, the uninformed, or the depraved.

In this account of persons with problems of identity, Olenka, Frank Abagnale, Tom Ripley, Walter Mitty, and Henry David Thoreau wanted to be others whom they admired. Only Abagnale and Ripley were conscious of being impostors. The others manifested unconscious yearnings.

Becoming effective is an important prerequisite for self-acceptance, and Thoreau's use of the jail experience to separate himself from Emerson, referred to above, demonstrates one way this may be accomplished.[14]

NOTES

1. Walter Harding, ed., *Thoreau as Seen by his Contemporaries* (New York: Dover, 1989), 62–63.

2. Ibid., 120.

3. Franklin B. Sanborn, *The Life of Henry David Thoreau*. Boston: Houghton Mifflin, 1917, 341–42.

4. Ibid.

5. Ralph Waldo Emerson, *Journals and Miscellaneous Notebooks*, various editors, 16 vols. (Cambridge: Harvard University Press 1960–), 8:498.

6. Harding, *Thoreau Contemporaries*, 73.

7. Ibid., 65.

8. Emerson 7:220–22. Cf. also note 14.

9. Henry David Thoreau, *Journal*. Bradford Torrey and Francis Allen, eds. New York: Dover, 1962, 3:6.

10. Ibid., 1:270.

11. Harding, *Days of Thoreau*, 8.

12. Lidian Emerson to Lucy Jackson Brown, Jan. 11, 1842, qtd. in Richard Lebeaux, *Young Man Thoreau* (Amherst: University of Massachusetts Press, 1977), 170–71.

13. Quoted in Harding, *Days of Thoreau*, 135.

14. For one summary of Thoreau's separation process, see R. Conrad, "Realizing Resistance: Thoreau and the First of August, 1846, at Walden," *The Concord Saunterer* 12/13 (2004–05), esp. 176–79.

Chapter Seven

Fyodor Dostoyevsky's Underground Man and the Psychogenesis of Stalking

TERRORISM AND STALKING

Terrorism may be defined as the threat of violence or its use to instill fear, which is intended to force an individual or group to pursue some goal—political, religious, economic, psychological, etc.

A common stereotype is that someone who commits these abhorrent acts—such as planting a bomb on an airliner, detonating a vehicle bomb on a city street, or tossing a grenade into a crowded sidewalk café—is abnormal. The argument that terrorism is pathological behavior minimizes the political or social issues that motivate terrorists to act. There is no evidence that terrorists, as a group, are diagnosable as psychopathic or otherwise clinically disturbed.

So-called normal people can be terrorists, and we are ourselves capable of terrorist acts under some circumstances. The atomic destruction of Hiroshima demonstrates that military forces are eminently capable of terrorism, killing noncombatants. Few suggest that the broad range of military forces involved in such killing must all be abnormal.

Acts of terrorism, however, do not come out of the clear blue sky. What has not been sufficiently recognized is that mortifying shame is its precipitant. The trajectory by which normal people become capable of terrorism is usually gradual, perhaps imperceptible to the individual, and involves humiliation.

Also insufficiently recognized is that traditional counterterrorist responses—retaliation and revenge—increase the underlying mortification and lead to an escalating cycle of terrorism.

Terrorism is a complex behavior and many factors are involved in the creation of a terrorist. A multidisciplinary approach is necessary to comprehend it.

Three cases of terrorism are presented in this and the following chapters—Dostoyevsky's fictional account of a stalker; a cyberterrorist whom I treated in connection with my work as a psychiatric consultant to the Middlesex (Mass.) Sheriff's Office; and Dr. Theodore Kaczynski (the "Unabomber"), with whom I have corresponded. All three were mortified by shame prior to engaging in their acts of terrorism.

DOSTOYEVSKY'S STALKER

Fyodor Dostoyevsky's (1821–1881) first major novel, *Notes from Underground* (1864), demonstrates his literary skill and psychological insight. Depicting the personality of a chronically shame-ridden, hypersensitive-but-defenseless person who becomes a stalker after an intensely humiliating experience, Dostoyevsky presents in minute detail the psychogenesis of stalking. This chapter explores the relationship of stalking to mortifying shame and possibly to underlying Asperger disorder.

Notes from Underground was written at a low point in Dostoyevsky's life. His literary journal, *Time,* had failed, his wife was ill and dying, he had financial problems, his politics were the subject of attacks by the press, and his epilepsy was worsening. Perhaps some of his personal feelings found their way into the novel. The novel's key metaphor, the "underground," describes a subterranean state of mind inhabited by a person without human connectedness, a defense against mortifying shame.

Dostoyevsky's Underground Man pays a price by isolating himself from human relationships. He describes the second-floor furnished room in which he dwells as "dismal" and "squalid," a "loathsome, stinking underground hole" on the outskirts of town. In it he ruminates over elaborate ways to get revenge on those who have humiliated him.

Stalking may be defined as repeated and persistent unwanted communications or approaches that produce fear in the victim. The stalker may telephone or follow an individual, or keep a residence under surveillance, intruding on the victim's privacy and invoking a fear of violence.

Most stalkers are not psychotic, although many suffer from mental disorders such as depression, substance abuse, or personality disorder. The stalker whom Dostoyevsky describes, a vindictive middle-aged man, is the author of the two-part diary comprising the novel. In the first part, he depicts his present life, cut off from family and friends. In part two, recounting the past, he reveals how he became the man we meet in the opening pages, a vengeful, help-rejecting hypochondriac:

I am a sick man. . . . I am a spiteful man. I am an unattractive man. I think my liver is diseased. Then again, I don't know a thing about my illness; I'm not even sure what hurts. I'm not being treated and never have been, though I respect both medicine and doctors. It's out of spite that I don't wish to be treated. . . . I won't really be able to explain to you precisely who will be hurt by my spite in this case; . . . if I refuse to be treated, it's out of spite.[1]

MORTIFYING SHAME

The mortifying episode occurs one evening in a seedy side of town when the Underground Man inadvertently blocks the path of a six-foot army officer who is trying to leave a tavern in haste. The Underground Man describes how the officer took hold of him by the shoulders and without a word of warning or explanation, moved him out of the way as though he were a stick of furniture. Already feeling "small and scrawny" like a human housefly, he states, "I could have forgiven even a beating, but I could never forgive his moving me out of the way and entirely failing to notice me." Feeling depersonalized, he leaves the tavern and goes straight home. Subsequently, whenever he notices the officer on the street he stares at him with hatred and malice and begins his obsessive pursuit. He learns the officer's name when a passerby calls it out. Bribing a doorman, he finds out where and with whom the officer lives.

The Underground Man decides to write a caricature of the officer, exposing and slandering him. The project fills him with delight, but never gets published. He finds this very annoying, and at times feels that he has "choked on spite."

After four years, he writes to the soldier, challenging him to a duel—but he leaves open the possibility of reconciliation. He has the fantasy that the officer could come running, hug him, and offer his friendship.

That would have been splendid! We would have led such a wonderful life! He would have shielded me with his; I would have ennobled him with my culture, and well, with my ideas.[2]

The Underground Man does not send the letter but instead encounters his enemy on St. Petersburg's Nevsky Prospect, where he frequently sees him, often making way for him. This time, he decides to hold his ground:

"Why is it you're always first to step aside?" I badgered myself in insane hysteria, at times waking up at three in the morning. . . . "What if I were to meet him and not step aside?"[3]

To be as presentable as possible in what he imagines will be a public scandal, the Underground Man decides to purchase a pair of black gloves, more *bon ton* than the lemon-colored ones he first considered, but he needs a salary advance to pay for them. He also needs a new overcoat because the one he owns is shabby. When he finally feels properly attired, however, the Underground Man finds it difficult to follow through on his plan:

> One time I'd fully resolved to do it but the result was that I merely stumbled and fell at his feet because, at the very last moment, only a few inches away from him, I lost my nerve. He stepped over me very calmly and I bounced to one side like a rubber ball.[4]

Finally, with his eyes closed, he advances at the lieutenant; they bump into each other, and the Underground Man doesn't yield an inch. The officer doesn't even turn around, pretending (in the Underground Man's mind) not to have noticed. At first the Underground Man feels triumphant, not having backed down. Returning home, he sings Italian arias. Soon, however, he realizes that once again he has been ineffectual.

He confronts his underlying mortifying shame with heroic dreams of glory:

> I believed blindly that by some kind of miracle, some external circumstance, everything would suddenly open up and expand . . . that I would suddenly step forth into God's world, almost riding on a white horse and wearing a laurel.[5]

No matter how glorious the daydreams, they do not help the Underground Man avoid the erosive effects of chronic mortifying shame. When we first encounter him on page 1 of his memoirs, its devastating effects are apparent. He is a forty-year-old, bitter, scornful, self-contradicting person, "mistrustful and sensitive as a hunchback or dwarf," living on the outskirts of the city. In a depersonalized, obsessive monologue, he states:

> There, in its disgusting, stinking underground, our offended, crushed, and ridiculed mouse immediately plunges into cold, malicious, and, above all, everlasting spitefulness. For forty years on end it will recall its insult down to the last, most shameful detail . . . add more shameful details . . . become ashamed of that fantasy.[6]

Deborah Martinsen makes some perceptive comments about the relationship of several of Dostoyevsky's short novels to the concept of shame that tie in well with the formulation presented in this essay.

> *Notes from Underground* is another Dostoevskian study in shame. While Golyadkin protects himself by splitting (being more observer than participant) and

the white nights dreamer by fantasizing [about approaching young women and telling them his story], Dostoyevsky's Underground Man intellectualizes.[7]

Martinsen notes that the Underground Man "writes partly to relieve his guilt, but he cannot—largely because he cannot escape the prison of his shame."[8] He reveals (she notes) that "he is ashamed of his emotional neediness, which he perceives as weakness. This revelation prepares readers for the narrator's narcissistic rages: He first lashes out at those who witness his weakness and then flagellates himself for expressing his anger. His inability to control his public image exacerbates his shame. . . [His shame] stifles his attempts to relieve his conscience."[9]

The Underground Man claims that "we are all fallen creatures, we are all ashamed of ourselves, we are all seeking to be other than who we are," and he attempts to alleviate his shame by sharing it, a strategy borrowed by Jean-Baptiste Clamence in Albert Camus' novel *The Fall*, which is discussed in the concluding portion of this book.

NOTES

1. Fyodor Dostoyevsky, *Notes from Underground*, Michael R. Katz, ed. (New York: Norton, 2001), 1.

2. Ibid., 35.

3. Ibid., 36.

4. Ibid., 37–38.

5. Ibid., 39.

6. Ibid., 8–9.

7. Deborah Martinsen, "Introduction," Dostoevsky, *Notes from Underground, the Double and Other Stories* (New York: Barnes & Noble, 2003), xxii-xxiii. The other novels referred to are *The Double* (1846) and *White Nights* (1848).

8. Ibid., xxiv.

9. Ibid., xxvi.

Chapter Eight

The Case of the Quadriplegic Cyberstalker

In the course of my work as psychiatric consultant to the Middlesex Sheriff's Office, I had the unusual opportunity to treat a young man, Mr. W., who had terrorized a community in Townsend, Massachusetts, on the Internet from his home in Smithville, Missouri. (The case was reported the *Boston Globe* in 2001.[1]) In terms of the mortifying shame that led to his act of terrorism, W. is the nonfictional counterpart of Dostoyevsky's nameless Underground Man.

Sixteen-year-old W., a high-school athlete and honor student, received a telephone call from a longstanding friend with whom he had been inseparable in childhood. They had spent many hours in the school band, on the soccer team, and in the Boy Scouts, where they hiked, swam, canoed, and did good deeds together.

The friend, T., who had just received his driver's license, wanted to take W. on a car trip to the local mall in his late-model Thunderbird. T. exceeded the speed limit on a winding, gravelly back road in the fog at dusk. He lost control of the car, which spun around and smashed into a tree on the passenger's side. Although T. emerged unhurt, the impact rendered W. quadriplegic. He had sustained an incomplete injury to his spinal cord, causing loss of motor activity in the lower extremities but allowing some movement in the arms and wrists.

Following the accident, T. discontinued all forms of communication with W., although they had been the best of friends since childhood. W. felt powerless and ineffective in his attempts to bring his friend back into his life and mortified by what he took as a betrayal of their years of camaraderie. T. did not answer his phone calls or letters. A year later, W. sued him, citing driving to endanger, but T. was under eighteen years old at the time of the accident, and thus considered below the age of legal accountability.

Although W. missed months of school, with tutoring, summer sessions, and an indomitable will, he graduated on time, on the honor roll, and won a college scholarship. He enrolled and began computer-science study.

Those who knew him were impressed by his perseverance, but he concealed inner pain. Activities he once enjoyed, such as dating or playing soccer, were no longer feasible. Unable to get out of bed by himself, his social life was curtailed. Despite hard work, intelligence, and the ministrations of loving parents, he was a bored quadriplegic teenager with time on his hands and no ready solution to the problems of loneliness and boredom that he experienced.

Turning his attention to the Internet, he began communicating with members of a chat room for the students of a middle school a thousand miles away. The younger students with whom he dialogued could not see that he was wheelchair-bound, and W. was freed from the identity of a cripple. Before long, he was spending eight hours a day online.

Eventually he blew his cover. Some of the chat-room youths noticed online slipups that W. had made, and demanded that he reveal his true identity. W. did not want to admit he was an invalid and insisted he belonged to the class at the middle school. Overwhelmed by anxiety lest they reject him (an anxiety conditioned by the rejection of his best friend), W. threatened to blow up the whole school unless his chat-room friends believed him.

What began as an attempt at self-restoration had turned into a source of disrespect and humiliation. The more W. went online, the more he felt humiliated. His shame rage intensified. He posted two photos on the chat room's web site: the school in the crosshairs of a rifle scope; and the school's principal, bleeding through simulated bullet holes in the head and chest. He also invoked the recent horrors of the Columbine High School massacre with the words: "Remembering those two heroes in Columbine: RIP Eric Harris and Dylan Klebold." Beneath a "hit list" of twenty-four eighth-graders and three of their teachers, he wrote: "Some of you lucky individuals will go home with more bullet holes in your body than you came with."

Before students and teachers arrived at school the next morning, police with bomb-sniffing dogs patrolled the hallways and inspected classrooms. Teachers searched student books and backpacks for suspicious items. Parents of youths on W.'s hit list did not allow their offspring to leave home, let alone attend school.

If W.'s goal was to invoke terror in the middle-school community, he attained it. Just six months after the Columbine tragedy, the threat of another school massacre hit home. The terrorist was a quadriplegic several states away, but as far as anyone in town knew, a potential killer was at bay.

AN ESCALATING CYCLE OF REVENGE

The steps in the progression of terrorism, beginning with the offer of a dusk ride on a dirt road, involve, as we have seen in this volume's Introduction, feelings of being powerless to rectify disrespect, mortification, shame rage, and revenge.

Powerlessness: Feelings of impotence constitute one of the crucial factors giving rise to terrorism. Professor Bruce Hoffman, adviser on counterterrorism to the U.S. Office of National Security Affairs, writes: "Terrorism is designed to create power where there is none or to consolidate power where there is very little."[2]

Dr. Gershen Kaufman, author and psychologist, notes that those who feel powerless identify with the aggressor: "Terrorism is essentially a strategy of the powerless. Groups who have felt decidedly powerless and humiliated for decades have reversed roles. The tormented now become tormentors."[3]

The crippling auto accident rendered W. physically powerless. This was compounded by psychical impotence that occurred when his once-inseparable friend abandoned him.

Disrespect: The human need to bond and be part of a group is strong. When one is disrespected, especially publicly, the connection to others is threatened. When W. was disrespected in the chat room, he felt marginalized. This opened the psychical wound caused by his friend's rejection. W. threatened violence to restore his place in the group.

Mortification: Feeling mortified, one's natural response is to retaliate. If this does not take place, the anger may be turned against oneself and depression may occur. W.'s first response was to retaliate. When first arrested by the police, he told them: "I'd like to slit my ex-friend's throat."[4]

Shame rage: There is no effective defense against shame as there is, for example, against guilt. It is possible to blame another if one feels guilty, but it is impossible to externalize and project shame. The emotion remains and becomes more and more intense.

Violent counterresponse: At a certain level of intensity, the urge to discharge shame rage curdles into a yearning for sweet revenge. The desire to even the score, however, causes others to retaliate, escalating the cycle of terrorism.

TREATMENT: RESTORING SELF-RESPECT

His disability had left W. feeling defective, but on the Internet, no one would know that he was paralyzed. In a chat room devoted to the band Limp Bizkit, he had met students from the Hawthorne Brooke Middle School and struck up a virtual friendship with the eighth-graders. W. tried to pretend he was one of them, but at length they didn't believe him. As when he had been avoided by T. after the accident, W. felt he had lost an important source of support, and felt ineffective in regaining it. When they continued to doubt that he was one of them, he responded by telling them that he was going to blow up the school.

Before beginning his visits to the middle-school chat room, W. stated, "What I was missing in my social life I discovered on the internet. I found those friends, and it made me feel good to be part of the community again. . . . Even though these friends were 1500 miles away and I had never seen them, I felt a strong connection and involvement with them. . . . When they started to disbelieve me, I threatened to kill them all."

In the host-vector model—a paradigm commonly used to analyze infectious diseases—the outcome of infection results from the virulence of the vector and the immunity of the host. This model may help explain why the response to disrespect and powerlessness varies from person to person and from group to group. People and groups who feel marginalized to begin with, as W. acknowledges he was before his act of terrorism, are more likely to be infected by the virus of disrespect, and less able to control their mortified outrage.

Frantz Fanon, the psychiatrist and author of *The Wretched of the Earth* (1961), a famous study of the effect of political colonization on a nation's psyche, wrote of the value of violence as a "cleansing force." In the words of a recent Fanon reader, "Even random violence against a perceived oppressor is seen as a redemptive act. It's a way for powerless people to feel in power, to feel that they can regain their self-respect, that they can take control of their lives."[5]

The violent response to violence is, at best, a temporary solution. Since both sides in a battle of terrorism feel mortified, further violence only exacerbates the viruses of disrespect and disempowerment.

I conducted biweekly psychiatric treatment sessions lasting from fifteen minutes to an hour in the prison infirmary during W.'s incarceration. The long-term treatment goals, restoring self-esteem and mental and spiritual empowerment, began with empathy.

It is not easy to experience what it feels like to be a quadriplegic. In order to enter that world more easily, I asked W. if he would be good enough to write a statement on the subject, "What It's Like to Be Me." In it, he described at length the daunting daily problems involved in such mundane matters as getting out of bed, putting on his clothes, and opening containers (with his mouth and left hand because of the right-hand paralysis).

Role-playing was a crucial therapeutic tool. By playing the part of W.'s former friend, I could share with him the guilt T. must have felt after the devastating accident that resulted from his speeding at dusk, in the fog, on a gravel road. Forgiveness is a powerful therapeutic tool. Ultimately, W. had to assume responsibility for accompanying the novice driver on his maiden voyage, and when he could do that, and forgive himself for doing so, he was gradually able to let go of the shame rage.

In the final months of treatment, we used the insights derived from therapy to write this report. W. felt great remorse about his crime but appreciated the opportunity to use it constructively in this article, which could empower others to better understand the psychodynamics of terrorism. It was an important part of his therapy. It was also therapeutic for him to realize that his stalwart approach to his quadriplegia made him an admirable person in my eyes, and would have a similar effect on others.

W. was paroled after serving six months of a one-year sentence. He returned to college, where he is not permitted to use the Internet. He has returned to the university community for further studies where, no longer feeling so worthless and abandoned, he has made friends and looks forward to a career as a teacher or guidance counselor. Those who have been hurt have the capacity to heal when they have learned to use their suffering in a constructive fashion. After spending years feeling worthless and abandoned, W. is at last looking forward with a greatly improved outlook on life.

NOTES

1. Michele Kurtz, "The 'Stalker' Who Stayed at Home: A Town Terrorized Over the Internet," *Boston Globe*, September 2, 2001.

2. Bruce Hoffmann, *Inside Terrorism* (New York: Columbia University Press, 1998), 44.

3. Gershen Kaufman, *Shame: The Power of Caring* (Rochester, Vt.: Shenkman Books, 1992), 229–30.

4. Qtd. in Kurtz, "'Stalker.'" All other quotes from W. are taken from my notes for my study "The Case of the Quadriplegic Cyberterrorist," *Current Psychiatry*, 2002.

5. Eva Bellin et al., "Understanding Terrorism." *Harvard Magazine* 104 (Jan.-Feb. 2002).

Chapter Nine

The Unabomber at Harvard: A Murderous Phoenix

Theodore John (Ted) Kaczynski, formerly a professor of mathematics, is an American terrorist convicted of murder for bomb mailings which killed three and wounded twenty-nine persons. Currently, he is incarcerated in a super-maximum security prison. He justified his crimes as a fight against the evils of technological "progress."

Because the FBI referred to him as the UNABOM ("university and airline bomber," to reflect where his first bombs exploded) before his identity was known, variants of that code name, including "Unabomer," "Unibomber," and "Unabomber," have been used.

Kaczynski has been compared to Joseph Conrad's character Adolf Verloc, a former university professor turned terrorist in *The Secret Agent* (1907). Kaczynski, who was quite familiar with the novel, occasionally signed his mail bombings "Conrad" or "Konrad." The Unabomber also bears a certain resemblance to Dostoyevsky's Underground Man, as we shall see.

In childhood, Kaczynski was unusually shy and aloof. This condition developed, according to his mother, after several weeks of hospitalization for an allergic reaction. His parents were not permitted to visit at the time, and when their son returned home they noted he was withdrawn and unresponsive to human contact.

He attended a nursery school where he was described as having "very strong ideas as to what he wants to do and how he wants to do it. He will not play with other children. He will play beside the others but does not want them interfering in anything he is doing."[1]

The older of two offspring of ambitious, self-educated parents, Kaczynski was rather reserved and bookish as a youngster. A neighbor described him as brilliant but unsociable:

He'd walk by without saying hello, just nothing. No other younger person in all
my years has ever done that. . . . The little boy just came home and descended
into the basement, and did his thing.[2]

His mother devoted herself to caring for her youngster, for example, by
holding him in her lap while reading *Scientific American* to him. He spent
considerable time alone in an attic room. When he heard a car drive up he'd
say, "There's so and so—don't call me down. I don't want to see them."
Following the birth of his younger brother in 1949, he seemed to withdraw
further, avoiding eye contact, refusing to speak, rarely smiling, and often
heading to the attic to be by himself.

In school, he skipped grades because of high test scores and remembers not
fitting in with the older children, who teased and verbally abused him. He had
no close friends. He enjoyed woodworking and chemistry, and described his
fascination with explosives in an essay, "How I blew up Howard Snilly."

Kaczynski was a National Merit finalist in high school and was accepted at
Harvard College at the age of sixteen. In his Harvard file, his mother wrote:

Much of his time is spent at home reading and contriving numerous gadgets
made of wood, string, tape, lenses, gears, wheels, etc., that test out various principles in physics. His table and desk are always a mess of test tubes, chemicals,
batteries, ground coal, etc. He will miss greatly, I think, this browsing and put-
tering in his messy makeshift lab.[3]

The messiness persisted at Harvard's Eliot House, where his room emit-
ted such a foul stench that the headmaster ordered him to clean it up. (Hans
Asperger, who delineated Asperger syndrome in 1944, noted that the child
suffering from it "stacks boxes full of useless junk. . . . There are serious rows
when the mother dares to throw anything away."[4])

As a student, Kaczynski in 1959–62 participated in psychological research on
the subject of stress devised by Professor Henry A. Murray of the Department
of Social Relations. Murray, researching two-person interactions (the "dyad"),
described the experimental procedure in *American Psychologist* (1963):

First, you are told you have a month in which to write a brief exposition of your
personal philosophy of life, an affirmation of the major guiding principles in
accord with which you live or hope to live your life. Second, when you return
to the Annex [Murray's workshop] with your finished composition, you are
informed that in a day or two you and a talented young lawyer will be asked to
debate the respective merits of your two philosophies.[5]

Murray did not tell the research subjects that they would be debating an
aggressive lawyer who was instructed to surprise, deceive, and ridicule them,

disputing the respective merits of their philosophies. A biographer of Kaczynski at Harvard wrote:

> As instructed, the unwitting subject attempted to represent and to defend his personal philosophy of life. Invariably, however, he was frustrated, and finally brought to expressions of real anger by the withering assault of his older, more sophisticated opponent while fluctuations in the subject's pulse and respiration were measured on a cardiotachometer.[6]

It is difficult to imagine a better way to humiliate, disrespect, and discredit another human being than by invalidating his or her philosophy of life, the major guiding principles by which that person lives. Kaczynski, however, denied that Murray's experiments had any important effect on his psyche:

> I experienced a lasting resentment of Murray and his co-workers. This resentment was not primarily due to the "dyadic disputation" that Chase makes so much of. What I mainly resented was the fact that I had been talked into participating in studies that involved extensive invasion of my privacy—and by people whom I disliked personally. I am quite confident that my experiences with Professor Murray had no significant effect on the course of my life.[7]

Perhaps the impact of Murray's deliberately disrespectful encounters had more of an effect on Kaczynski's psyche than he realized. He told a court-appointed psychiatrist, Dr. Sally Johnson, who conducted competency hearings prior to his trial in 1998, that while he was at the University of Michigan, where he was studying for a doctoral degree in mathematics, he began having nightmares, which continued for several years:

> In the dream I would feel either that organized society was hounding me with accusation in some way, or that organized society was trying in some way to capture my mind and tie me down psychologically or both. In the most typical form some psychologist or psychologists (often in association with parents or other minions of the system) would either be trying to convince me that I was "sick" or would be trying to control my mind through psychological techniques. . . . I would grow angrier and finally I would break out in physical violence against the psychologist and his allies. At the moment when I broke out into violence and killed the psychologist or other such figure, I experienced a great feeling of relief and liberation.[8]

In his fifth year at Michigan, Kaczynski envisioned having a sex-change operation and made an appointment to see the Health Center psychiatrist, but he ultimately could not bring himself to talk about the subject and left feeling "rage, shame and humiliation."[9] He explained the problem to Dr. Johnson:

> I felt disgusted about what my uncontrolled sexual cravings had almost led me to do and I felt humiliated, and I violently hated the psychiatrist. Just then there came a major turning point in my life. Like a Phoenix, I burst from the ashes of my despair to a glorious new hope; I thought I wanted to kill that psychiatrist because the future looked utterly empty to me. I felt I wouldn't care if I died.[10]

The murderous "phoenix" told Dr. Johnson that subsequently he began having fantasies in which he would avenge himself against a society he increasingly perceived as evil, obsessively enforcing conformity through psychological manipulation. He believed that the wish for sex-change surgery stemmed from a desire to please others—parents, school authorities, and math-department professors who had brought him to the point of contemplating self-emasculation.

In 1967, Kaczynski received a prize for his doctoral thesis from the University of Michigan, and he moved to the University of California to teach mathematics the following year. His aloofness and lack of involvement with students was reflected in their low ratings of him. He resigned in 1969, relocated to a remote shack in Lincoln, Montana, and lived a simple life on the little money he earned from occasional jobs and financial support from his family.

Kaczynski had an encounter with a woman that in several respects was similar to the Underground Man's mishap with Lisa in Dostoyevsky's novella, which we will discuss in the next section. He took the woman to dinner and two weeks later invited her to pick apples with him and make a pie of them in his parent's home. On their second date she told him, "I do not wish to see you on a social basis."[11]

Soon after, Kaczynski composed an insulting limerick about her, which he posted throughout the factory where she worked. His brother, David, the factory manager, warned him to stop or he'd lose his job; Theodore persisted and, after posting the obscene limerick directly in front of David's desk, he was fired.

Beginning in May 1978, Kaczynski started mailing bombs to various people and continued to do so for the next eighteen years. Discussing the impact of Professor Murray's research on the student's subsequent behavior, a Kaczynski biographer theorizes:

> Kaczynski's Harvard experiences shaped his anger and legitimized his wrath. By graduation, all the elements that would ultimately transform him into the Unabomber were in place; the ideas out of which he would construct a philoso-

phy; . . . Within four years after leaving Harvard his life's plan would be firmly fixed.[12]

In order to understand this profound impact, it is helpful to consider in more detail a constellation of symptoms that the Austrian pediatrician Hans Asperger first noted in a group of youngsters referred to him because of behavioral problems involving aggression, malice, and violence. In the next chapter (which concludes this section on stalking), the Unabomber's problems are explored in connection with Dostoyevsky's Underground Man, who may be considered his fictional counterpart.

NOTES

1. Robert Graysmith, *Unabomber: A Desire to Kill* (Washington DC: Regnery, 1997), 52.

2. Ibid., 50.

3. Ibid.

4. Hans Asperger, *"Autistic Psychopathy" in Children* [1944], in Uta Frith, ed., *Autism and Asperger Syndrome* (London: Cambridge University Press, 1991), 82.

5. Qtd. in Alston Chase, *Harvard and the Unabomber: The Education of an American Terrorist* (New York: Norton, 2003), 232–33.

6. Ibid., 233.

7. T. Kaczynski, letter to the author, Nov. 20, 2005.

8. Chase, 304.

9. Ibid., 305.

10. Ibid., 305–06.

11. Graysmith, 24.

12. Chase, 294.

Chapter Ten

The Unabomber, the Underground Man, and Asperger Syndrome

"AUTISTIC ACTS OF MALICE"

Hans Asperger (1906–1980), delineating the syndrome he identified, called attention to "autistic acts of malice" among those whom he characterized as "little professors" because of the formal way in which they spoke, devoid of feeling:

> These acts typically appear to be calculated. With uncanny certainty, the children manage to do whatever is the most unpleasant or hurtful in a particular situation. . . . There can sometimes be distinctly sadistic acts. Delight in malice, which is rarely absent, provides almost the only occasion when the lost glance of these children appears to light up.[1]

The gratuitous maliciousness in Dostoyevsky's Underground Man is addressed by Nikolai Mikhailovski, a literary scholar:

> The underground man actually begins to torment Lisa for absolutely no reason at all; it is simply because she happened to be at hand. There are no reasons for his spite towards her. . . . The hero torments her because he wants or likes to torment. . . . There is an unconditional cruelty.[2]

It is likely that the Underground Man's cruelty is multi-determined and that his responses to Lisa involve unconscious displacement of hostility remaining from his previous encounters with schoolmates and the lieutenant. The intensity of the hostility, however, is analogous to those with Asperger disorder.

One seven-year-old boy whom Asperger studied told his mother:

44

Mummy, I shall take a knife one day and push it into your heart, then blood will spurt out. . . . It would be nice if I were a wolf. Then I could rip apart sheep and people, and then blood would flow.[3]

Theodore Kaczynski's sadistic malice was expressed when he described how he "blew to bits" Hugh Scrutton, a computer-rental store owner: "Excellent. Humane way to eliminate somebody. He probably never felt a thing."[4]

Asperger considered that such responses stemmed from the profound humiliation experienced by the stigmatized child:

Autistic children are often tormented and rejected by their classmates simply because they are different and stand out from the crowd. Their conduct, manner of speech and, not least, often grotesque demeanor cries out to be ridiculed. Children in general have a good eye for this and show great accuracy in their mocking of conspicuous character peculiarities. Thus, in the playground or on the way to school one can often see an autistic child at the center of a jeering horde of little urchins. The child himself may be hitting out in blind fury or crying helplessly.[5]

As mentioned in the previous section, in his first year as an undergraduate at Harvard, Kaczynski came to the conclusion that he needed sex-change surgery and scheduled an appointment with the campus psychiatrist to arrange it, but was unable to discuss this when the time came. He stated:

As I walked away from the building afterwards, . . .I said to myself why not really kill the psychiatrist and anyone else whom I hate? What is important is not the words that ran through my mind but the way I felt about them. What was entirely new was the fact that I really felt I could kill someone. My very hopelessness had liberated me because I no longer cared about death. I no longer cared about consequences and I said to myself that I really could break out of my rut in life an[d] do things that were daring, irresponsible or criminal.[6]

Dostoyevsky's Underground Man also describes feelings of humiliation in his early years, and, like Kaczynski, used his considerable intellect unsuccessfully to make connections with people:

My schoolmates received me with spiteful and pitiless jibes because I wasn't like any of them. But I couldn't tolerate their jibes; I couldn't possibly get along with them as easily as they got along with each other. . . . In order to avoid their jibes, I began to study and made it to the top of the class. . . . Their jibes ceased, but their hostility remained, and the relations between us became cold and strained. . . . As the years went by I made several attempts to get closer to

some of them; but these attempts always turned out to be unnatural and ended
of their own account.[7]

Not all acts of cruelty and malice, such as stalking and terrorism, are
indicative of Asperger syndrome, but when such acts arise, Asperger syndrome should be among the possible underlying problems that may produce
them. Recently, three forensic psychiatrists at the University of California
School of Medicine, came to a similar conclusion.[8] They note that Kaczynski was aloof and could not understand the feelings of others. He also
exhibited an aversion to being touched and experienced extreme distress
when exposed to noise, both common reactions in children with autism. A
neighbor described the young Kaczynski as "a child who was an old man
before his time," consistent with Hans Asperger's description of his young
patients as "little professors." And, as an adult, Kaczynski was extremely
impaired in social relationships.

Kaczynski's preoccupations with bomb-making and the perceived evils
of technology, the authors say, may be viewed as typical of the obsessive
interests of a person with Asperger syndrome. In their study cited above,
the University of California researchers conclude that their characterization of a subset of serial killers as having high-functioning autism could
lead to a greater understanding of the etiology of both serial homicide and
autism:

> Psychological phenomena of central importance to understanding serial killers
> such as deficits in empathy have frequently been explained as originating from a
> psychopathic core, thereby missing the possibility that deficits in empathy may
> also be due to autistic psychopathology.[9]

It makes sense to consider Asperger as a spectrum disorder. Its incidence
in the population at large is far greater than is thought. The major problem
is a difficulty "reading people," and those with the disorder are frequently
hurt by those who misread them. As a consequence, they may become social
isolates like the Underground Man and Kaczynski. Just as it is possible to
teach people how to have a dialogue with themselves (by writing a poem,
painting a picture, or playing a musical instrument) it is possible to teach
a person who has no concept of another's mind how to be in better touch
with people.

Until that occurs, there is bound to be considerable frustration, aggression,
and, at times, acts of violence on the part of those cut off from meaningful
contact with others, and these feelings will manifest in such problems as
stalking.

NOTES

1. Asperger, *"Autistic Psychopathy,"* 77.

2. Nikolai Mikhailovski, "Dostoevsky's Cruel Talent," quoted in Dostoevsky, *Notes from Underground*, Michael R. Katz, ed. (New York: Norton, 2001), 141–42.

3. Asperger, 79–80.

4. Quoted in Chase, 66.

5. Asperger, 79.

6. Chase, 305–06. Note that Tom Ripley's decision to murder Dickie Greenleaf arises after he feels humiliated about being called "queer."

7. Dostoevsky, *Notes from Underground* (2001), 46–47.

8. J. Arturo Silva, Michelle M. Ferrari, and Gregory B. Leong, "Asperger's disorder and the origins of the Unabomber," *American Journal of Forensic Psychiatry,* 24:2, (2003), 5–43.

9. Ibid.

Chapter Eleven

Chekhov's "The Man in a Case": Laughter that Killed

MORTIFICATION, RESILIENCE, AND TRANSFORMATION

It is a devastating experience to feel mortified by shame. Our next chapters examine the varied psychology of mortification.

Chekhov's Byelikov ("The Man in a Case") returns home, removes from his bedside table a picture of the woman whom he loved but who had, he felt, humiliated him, climbs into bed and does not leave it alive.

Glenn Gould retreats into a glass enclosed recording studio and never again performs publicly after feeling humiliated by Leonard Bernstein.

Conrad's title character in his novel *Lord Jim* moves further and further into the jungle to escape from guilt and shame, which pursue him wherever he goes.

Gabriel Conroy, in Joyce's "The Dead," drifts off into what appears to be psychological death resulting from a humiliating triangle between himself, his wife Gretta, and Gretta's dead lover.

Resilient people are able to thrive, mature, and increase competence in the face of adversity and it is always possible to develop this capability. We see this in Silvio, in Pushkin's "The Shot," who is mortified by shame during a duel, yet resists the temptation to get revenge. Instead of acting impulsively, he waits and demonstrates forbearance, developing resilience and magnanimity in the process. Unfortunately, Pushkin, unable to apply what he describes in his story to his own life, and feeling humiliated by a rival for his wife's affections, died in a duel.

"THE MAN IN A CASE"

As we have seen in "The Darling," Anton Chekhov (1860–1904) combines in his masterful fiction the sharp-eyed, nonjudgmental objectivity in which he was trained as a physician with the insight and compassion of a great artist. Not much external action takes place in his stories and plays as he holds up a mirror to ordinary life, but the apparent trivialities of everyday lives lead to profound psychological revelations.

The main action of "The Man in a Case," for example, occurs when the antihero, Byelikov, tumbles down a flight of stairs in his bulky galoshes, thudding on each step as he falls. Although physically unhurt, he is literally mortified by shame when his girlfriend, who unexpectedly appears, breaks out into startled laughter. Those peals of laughter literally kill him.

The narrator, Burkin, states: "This was more dreadful to Byelikov than anything else. I believe he would rather have broken his neck or both legs."[1] After touching his nose to see whether his glasses were on right, he returns home, goes to bed, and never again rises. A month later he dies.

Byelikov, an unusually orderly man and a strict disciplinarian, does everything in life properly to avoid any impropriety. He is presented as a case in point of "a not uncommon type." In this story within a story (a case within a case within a case) Burkin tells his friend Ivan:

> There are plenty of people in the world, solitary by temperament, who try to retreat into their shell like a hermit crab or a snail. Perhaps it is an instance of atavism, a return to the period when the ancestor of man was not yet a social animal and lived alone in his den or perhaps it is only one of the diversities of human character—who knows?[2]

Chekhov provides a vivid description of his protagonist, a personality type hypersensitive to ridicule and humiliation, who layers his clothes and encases his personal items so that he and his possessions are as protected as possible:

> He is remarkable for always wearing galoshes and a warm wadded coat, and carrying an umbrella even in the very finest weather, and his umbrella was in a case, and his watch was in a case made of grey chamois leather, and when he took out his penknife to sharpen his pencil, his penknife, too, was in a little case; and his face seemed to be in a case, too, because he always hid it in his turned-up collar. He wore dark spectacles and flannel vests, stuffed up

his ears with cotton-wool, and when he got into a cab always told the driver to put up the hood.[3]

Chekhov, an insightful psychologist, gets to the underlying psychodynamics:

The man displayed a constant and insurmountable impulse to wrap himself in a covering, to make himself, so to speak, a case which would isolate him and protect him from external influences.[4]

The reason for this, Burkin makes clear, is that

Actuality irritated him, frightened him, kept him in a state of continual agitation, and, perhaps to justify his timidity, his aversion for the present, he would always laud the past and things that had never existed, and the dead languages that he taught were in effect for him the same rubbers and umbrella in which he sought concealment from real life.[5]

FALLING IN LOVE AND A FALL DOWN THE STAIRS

Teaching school is an ordeal for Byelikov. He feels vulnerable to ridicule and becomes downcast and pale when students swarm around him, invading his personal space.

After school it is not easier because Byelikov considers it his duty to "maintain good relations with his colleagues" and goes about this in a controlling fashion. He will call on a teacher, sit down, and remain silent as if trying to detect something. After an hour or two spent in this fashion he leaves, thus avoiding the possibility of intimacy and its risks of humiliation.

Byelikov's fellow teachers despise being "under his thumb," and are afraid of him. To retaliate, they arrange a date for him with Varinka, the sister of the new geography teacher, Kovalenkov. She has a particular characteristic, not uncommon among Ukrainian women (we are told), which turns out to be Byelikov's undoing—her propensity to laugh. At the slightest provocation, she will burst out into peals of laughter.

Varinka is fond of Byelikov and gives him a photo of herself, which he places by his bed, and he opens his heart to her affections. Unfortunately, a mischievous practical joker draws a caricature of Byelikov, capturing his essence. He is depicted wearing galoshes with pants tucked in, carrying an umbrella, and with Varinka on his arm; the lampoon is captioned, "Anthropos in love."

This depiction, widely circulated among school teachers and administrators, pains him greatly. His face becomes "gloomier than a rain cloud," his lips quiver, and he mutters about the malicious, ill-natured people in the world.

Shocked, he returns home and the next day skips school for the first time ever. Nervously rubbing his hands together, twitching, and wrapping himself warmly although it is practically summer, he eats nothing and trudges off to visit Kovalenkov and Varinka.

She is not home and her brother, just awaking from a nap and cranky, coldly offers him a seat. After ten minutes of sitting in silence, Byelikov begins:

> I have come to you to relieve my mind. . . . Some malicious fellow has drawn a caricature of me and of another person who is close to both of us. . . . I have given no grounds for such an attack — on the contrary, I have always behaved as a respectable person would.[6]

They digress to another topic. Voices rise, Byelikov turns pale, objects to his colleague's tone of voice, flies into a nervous flutter, and threatens to speak of the other's rudeness to the principal. Kovalenkov seizes him from behind by the collar, gives him a push, and Byelikov tumbles downstairs with his galoshes thudding.

As he falls, Varinka enters with two lady friends who stand below staring. This is more humiliating to Byelikov than anything imaginable. Now the entire town would hear of it and there would be yet another caricature.

Varinka, seeing his ridiculous face and crumpled overcoat and galoshes, is unable to restrain herself. She emits peals of laughter loud enough to be heard in the other apartments: "Ha-ha-ha!" And this pealing, Burkin relates, is "the last straw that put an end to everything: to the proposed match, and to Byelikov's earthly existence."[7]

Byelikov returns home, removes Varinka's picture from the table, goes to bed, and never again rises. He remains there silently, answering only "yes" or "no" to questions posed, and dies a month later. In the coffin he appears to have an agreeable, even cheerful mien, as though he is glad he has finally found a case in which he could remain.

There is no effective defense against shame. Byelikov futilely attempts to insulate himself with layers of clothing and encasements, well aware of his hypersensitivity to shame.

His rigid attempts to control himself and others has a widespread effect on the community, according to Burkin, who exclaims:

> This little man, who always wore rubbers and carried an umbrella, had the whole high school under his thumb for fully fifteen years! The high school? The whole town! Our ladies did not get up private theatricals on Saturdays for fear

he would find it out, and the clergy dared not eat meat in Lent or play cards in his presence. Under the influence of people like Byelikov the whole town spent ten to fifteen frightened years. We were afraid to speak out loud, to write letters, to make acquaintances, to read books, to help the poor, to teach people how to read and write.[8]

Byelikov's need to dominate and control others, his galoshes and layers of clothing, the dead languages he teaches, the method he uses to "maintain good relations with colleagues," and his reclusive lifestyle are attempts to avoid the mortifying shame that ultimately kills him.

NOTES

1. Anton Chekhov, *Portable Chekhov*, 367.
2. Ibid., 355.
3. Ibid.
4. Ibid.
5. Ibid., 355–56.
6. Ibid., 365.
7. Ibid., 368.
8. Ibid., 357.

Chapter Twelve

Glenn Gould:
The "Cased-in Man" Syndrome

Glenn Gould (1932–1982) was a brilliant pianist whose recordings, particularly of Bach, demonstrate deep feeling, finger-work precision, clarity of counterpoint, rhythmic dynamism, and musical originality.

He was an unusual musician who would hum along while playing, conduct using his hand as if he were a solo instrumentalist, and rock and sway during performances. He eschewed handshaking, and prior to performances soaked his hands up to the arms in hot water. Gould played with fingers flat and outstretched, rather than curved, which he felt enabled him to play at a faster tempo, with greater precision. For this purpose, he sat in a low-slung chair his father built, positioning him at the right height for the flat-finger technique.

Outside our solar system, two American NASA space probes, *Voyager 1* and *Voyager 2*, launched in the late 1970s, fly toward other worlds. Each carries a metal, long-playing record constructed to last thousands of millennia, accompanied by a needle and a diagram that shows how to rotate and at what speed to play the disk. Each disk contains a sample of Earthian music, voices, and sounds. On each, there are portions of Glenn Gould playing a Bach Brandenburg Concerto.

The choice of Gould to represent the planet Earth in outer space is an indication that, despite his eccentricity and the controversy surrounding him, he is considered one of the twentieth century's outstanding classical musicians.

A prodigy who could read musical notation at the age of three years, he began composing at six, made his musical debut in Canada (where he was born) at fifteen and first performed publicly in the United States at age twenty-three. Soon after, he recorded Bach's *Goldberg Variations*, a piece with which he identified, calling it the "Gouldberg Variations."

At the age of forty-nine, Gould rerecorded the piece, having come to the realization that the variations were not separate and distinct, but had an underlying unity and formed a whole. He also became aware that he needed to play the piece more "deliberately," and increased the playing time of each variation.

A perfectionist, Gould used the latest reel-to-reel, multitrack technology, splicing out imperfections in his performance. Soon after completing the second version (he rarely ever rerecorded), Gould died from a brain hemorrhage.

Although the most proximal cause of death was long-standing, chronic hypertension, it could be said that Gould considered that his raison d'être was to create a recording worthy of Bach's masterpiece and that, once he accomplished this, his life's work was completed.

GLENN GOULD AND CHEKHOV'S BYELIKOV

At the age of thirty-two years, Gould left the concert hall permanently, feeling that he had been treated as a vaudevillian. He became a studio-recording artist, and never again gave a public performance. The reasons Gould chose the total isolation of the recording studio are similar to the ones leading the character Byelikov, after his fall, back to the privacy of his own home.

Based on the modus vivendi of Chekhov's Byelikov, we may delineate a syndrome, the "cased-in man" syndrome, which applies equally well to Gould. Gould's recording studio may be likened to the "cases" of his fictional counterpart. Thinking of Gould, the words of Chekhov's narrator, Burkin, come to mind: "There are plenty of people in the world, solitary by temperament, who try to retreat into their shell like a hermit crab or a snail."[1]

THE CASED-IN MAN SYNDROME

Gould and Byelikov, Chekhov's protagonist, share in common a number of characteristics: 1) a preoccupation with heavy clothing, which covers much of the body even on the warmest days—hat, ear muffs, winter overcoat, sweaters, and gloves; 2) a predilection for solitude; 3) the presence of inordinate anger, which may be turned inward; 4) a need for control; 5) mortifying shame; and 6) the need for encasements.

An Overabundance of Clothing

Gould's preoccupation with clothing is apparent in a joke he told about a man who consulted a psychoanalyst regarding a sexual problem. After a half year of treatment, the analyst announced, "I haff solved your problem. You are in love with your raincoat." The patient was indignant:

> "Five months of analysis! And $5,000 in fees! And you tell me I'm in love with my raincoat! That's *ridiculous*." Gould's voice dropped to a lower register. He began fingering the sleeve of his own raincoat. "Still," he said thoughtfully, "I *am* very fond of my raincoat."[2]

Although laughter is the best medicine, humor did not rid Gould of an obsession with clothing, described by Joseph Roddy, a profiler of Gould in the *New Yorker* magazine:

> It was not a cold day, but Gould was wearing a beret, ear muffs, a scarf, an overcoat, and a pair of sturdy leather mittens. In the restaurant, when he had peeled these off, he was still wearing a thick woolen shirt, a heavy sweater, a shaggy tweed sports jacket, woolen slacks, overshoes, and a pair of knit gloves from which the fingers had been cut.[3]

A musician with whom Gould had collaborated could have also been describing Byelikov when he wrote:

> I let into my hotel room a very odd individual muffled up in a sizeless overcoat and wearing cap, scarves, gloves and overshoes despite the hot weather outside.[4]

Gould and Byelikov both wrapped themselves up in their work as they did in their garments. Music, to Gould, was like Byelikov's Latin and Greek. Gould stated, "I was determined to wrap myself up in music because I found it was a damned good way of avoiding my schoolmates, with whom I did not get along."[5]

A Predilection for Solitude

"Even as a child Glenn was isolated," his next-door neighbor, Robert Fulford, the Canadian author, states of his same-age friend. Gould acknowledged being a social isolate, saying, "I opted out creatively."

By his late thirties, according to a Columbia recording director, Gould was "largely a recluse, seeing few people, centering his life on recordings, radio and TV shows and numerous articles. Direct human contact was not his strong suit."

Gould was fascinated by those who lived apart from others, and he produced a radio documentary, "The Solitude Trilogy," describing different forms of isolation—geographical, political, cultural, and religious. It consists of *The Idea of the North* (about northern Canada); *The Latecomers* (Newfoundland); and *The Quiet in the Land* (concerning the Mennonites).

The values espoused in the first of the three parts—elusiveness, strength of character, moral rectitude, and adherence to laws—correspond with both Byelikov's and Gould's values. Both were also uncomfortable with values that Gould attributed to the Mediterranean peoples—bright colors, displays of passion, and personal revelations.

Most likely Gould suffered from what is called "social phobia," and for him school, with its inevitable social interactions, was distinctly unpleasant. Gould wrote: "I found going to school a most unhappy experience and I got along miserably with most of my teachers and all of my fellow students."[6] He literally counted each second until lunch hour (10,000 seconds at 9 a.m., 9,900 at 9:15 a.m.) and prayed that nothing might happen to humiliate him.

Like Nathaniel Hawthorne's protagonist Wakefield (whom we shall meet in Chapter 20), both Gould and Byelikov were observers, rarely participating in the give-and-take of interpersonal relationships and friendship. Gould's lengthy telephone calls were not conversations but one-sided monologues, like the narratives of Jean-Baptiste Clamence in Albert Camus' *The Fall* (which are discussed in Chapter 33) and the nameless antihero of Dostoyevsky's *Notes from Underground*.

Inordinate Anger

Mortified by rage, Byelikov's anger against Varinka for her humiliating laughter was turned against himself and led to his psychological death. Gould did not always turn his anger against himself. Grabbing a school bully by the lapel on one occasion, he warned: "If you ever come near me again, I will kill you."[7] It may be that anger toward his overprotective mother was displaced onto the bully. A recording technician with whom Gould closely worked reported that at the height of his rage, Gould acknowledged that he was capable of inflicting bodily harm on his mother—perhaps even committing murder.

A Need for Control

Like Byelikov, Gould had a great need to control others, and thereby avoid being humiliated. He refused all interviews unless he knew in advance the questions that would be posed and often proposed the questions himself. "It was the need for control that made him conduct most of these interviews by means of the telephone and the tape recorder," a biographer writes.[8] In the recording studio and on the concert-hall stage, Gould insisted on having the last word; for example, he would decide where the microphones would be placed or the tempo of a piece. In fact, this need for control created a momentous problem with another controlling person, the composer and conductor Leonard Bernstein.

Although Gould's encounter with Bernstein was less disastrous than Byelikov's with Varinka, it was the culmination of many years of humiliation and led to the end of the era of Gould's public performances. Soon after this incident, Gould entered the glass-cased recording studio.

The bone of contention between Gould and Bernstein was the tempo for their performance of the Brahms D-minor Piano Concerto. Gould wanted to play the slow movement very slowly and shared his enthusiasm for this idea with Bernstein who said, "Of course, you're exaggerating. You're not going to really do it this way. You're just showing me what you've found, with these mathematical relationships between one movement and another." Gould, however, was adamant: "No, this is the way we'll play it." He acknowledged a "spinal resilience" when confronted with opinions not his own.

Bernstein objected but capitulated. Before the performance, however, he stepped onstage and in a mellifluous voice disaffiliated himself from Gould's aesthetic judgment, stating that it would be "a rather—shall we say—unorthodox performance . . . a performance distinctly different from any I've heard, or even dreamt of, for that matter."

Raising the question of why he would involve himself in a project of which he disapproved, Bernstein explained that it was out of curiosity, to experiment, and for adventure. When he told the audience that the only other time he had "had to submit to a soloist's wholly new and incompatible concept [was] the last time I accompanied Mr. Gould," the laughter was pronounced. Gould, waiting in the wings to perform, had to endure it all.[9]

Mortifying Shame

Humiliation, especially in public, about a heartfelt matter is quite intense. A psychologist writes, "To be exposed and laughed at for something which . . . is trivial is . . . to be distinguished from exposure to a part of myself which I hold to be very dear, even essential to my inner well-being."[10] Clearly, Gould considered that his musical judgments were very important. Indeed, they were essential to his well-being. He lived for music and it would have been difficult to make a distinction between him and it.

Gould's public humiliation was reinforced by *New York Times* music critic Harold Schonberg's review of the concert: "The reason [Gould] plays it so slow is maybe his technique is not so good." Other reviews over the years were equally humiliating. The *Chicago News* wrote: "Music's most successful hipster, Glenn Gould, finally slouched onto the Orchestra Hall stage after three cancellations. . . . Seating himself at the Ouija board on a sawed-off rickety relic of a chair that was held together with wires, the disheveled recit-alist sang and stomped and conducted."[11]

It offended Gould greatly that he, not the music he interpreted, was the focus of concert-hall attention. The state of ecstasy in which he liked playing required a loss of self-consciousness, which the audience and critics disrupted. He wrote Eugene Ormandy, conductor of the Philadelphia Orchestra, "I can only describe to you a great apprehension in regard to giving concerts in Philadelphia. . . . I have come to feel something approaching terror at the thought of playing."[12] Fortunately, while still a young man, Gould discovered the recording studio as an alternative to the concert hall.

The Need for Encasement: The Recording Studio

Gould's recording studio was analogous to the encasements of his fictional counterpart Byelikov, which, Chekhov wrote, "sheltered [him] from real life." The pianist noted that early in life,

> [i]n the privacy, the solitude of the studio (and if all Freudians will stay clear) the womb-like security of the studio, it was possible to make music in a more direct, more personal manner than the concert hall would permit. I had decided that there was something just a little bit degrading about giving concerts. The process was essentially distasteful. I fell in love with broadcasting that day. For me the microphone has never been that hostile, clinical, inspiration-sapping analyst some critics, fearing it, complain about . . . . That day, in 1950, it became and [has] remained a friend.[13]

By splicing out errors and dubbing in segments from superior "takes," Gould was able to create the sound he heard in his mind's ear. Above all, the recording studio gave him total control over the performance. Living remote from the world of people, he interacted with it electronically.

NOTES

1. Chekhov, *Portable Chekhov*, 355.

2. Jock Carroll, *Glenn Gould: Some Portraits of the Artist as a Young Man* (Toronto: Stoddart, 1995), 17.

3. John McGreevy, ed., *Glenn Gould by Himself and his Friends* (Toronto: Doubleday, 1983), 113.

4. Ibid., 298.

5. Otto Friedrich, *Glenn Gould: A Life and Variations* (New York: Random House, 1989), 29–30.

6. Geoffrey Payzant, *Glenn Gould: Music and Mind* (Toronto: Van Nostrand, 1987), 3.

7. Friedrich, 23.

8. Ibid., 296.

9. Ibid., 103–04.

10. Gershen Kaufman, *Shame: The Power of Caring.* Cambridge: Shenkman, 1985, 104.

11. Both in Friedrich, 106–07.

12. Ibid., 94.

13. Payzant, 36.

Chapter Thirteen

Homophobic Dysphoria in Annie Proulx's *Brokeback Mountain*

POST-TRAUMATIC STRESS
AND INTERNALIZED HOMOPHOBIA

Brokeback Mountain, the short story by Annie Proulx (1935–) which was adapted into Ang Lee's award-winning motion picture, is about two itinerant ranch hands, Ennis del Mar and Jack Twist (played in the film by Heath Ledger and Jake Gyllenhaal), who meet and fall in love in their late teens on a sheepherding job on Brokeback Mountain in Wyoming. Elaborating on the original short story, the film documents in painstaking detail the vicissitudes of their complex, tragic relationship over the next two decades.

When they first begin work, Ennis is stationed at the base camp while Jack watches after the sheep higher on the mountain. They initially meet only for meals at the base camp, where they gradually become friends. After a time they exchange jobs, with Jack taking over duties at the foot of the mountain and Ennis tending the flock above.

One night, after sharing a bottle of whiskey, Ennis decides to remain at the base overnight instead of returning to the mountain. He is at first reluctant to sleep in the same tent as Jack, but late that night the men share a brief, intense sexual encounter. During the rest of the summer their sexual and emotional relationship deepens further, set against the open vistas of the Big Horn Mountains of eastern Wyoming, in Ang Lee's spacious film.

At the end of the summer they part. Monosyllabic mostly, once Ennis says, "I'm no queer." Jack replies, "Me neither. A one-shot thing. Nobody's business but ours."[1] They are, however, unable to get over their love for each other.

Both men marry heterosexually, but, unable to be open about their homosexual relationship, Ennis and Jack settle for infrequent encounters on "fishing trips" which they tell their wives they are taking. They don't fish, but enjoy each other's company and their wilderness surroundings, which symbolize their freedom.

Ennis tells Jack about a scene he saw as a boy: "There was these two old guys ranched together down home, Earl and Rich—Dad would pass a remark when he seen them. They was a joke, even though they was pretty tough old birds. I was what, nine years old and they found Earl dead in a irrigation ditch. They'd took a tire iron to him, spurred him up, drug him around by his dick until it pulled off, just bloody pulp."[2]

His father made sure he saw it, and the shocking event left Ennis with post-traumatic stress disorder, and he is hardly able to get the words out to talk about it. When Ennis was taught to hate homosexuality, he was taught to hate his own feelings, and himself. Years after first making love with Jack on a Wyoming mountainside, after his marriage has failed, after his world has been compressed into a mobile home, he still feels the pain, but projects it, blaming his partner in these telling words from the film: "Why don't you let me be? It's because of you, Jack, that I'm like this— nothing."

HOMOPHOBIC DYSPHORIA

Homophobic dysphoria—the anxiety, shame, and malaise occasioned by homosexuality—is evident in *Brokeback Mountain.*

A review in the *Los Angeles Times* describes the film as

[a] deeply felt, emotional love story that deals with the uncharted, mysterious ways of the human heart just as so many mainstream films have before it. The two lovers here just happen to be men.[3]

Although the film is, indeed, a deeply felt love story, the statement that the two lovers "just happen to be men" overlooks the extraordinary problem of being gay in our society. In a piece in *The New York Review of Books*, Daniel Mendelsohn makes this explicit:

Brokeback Mountain is about the specifically gay phenomenon of the "closet"— about the disastrous emotional and moral consequences of erotic self-repression and of the social intolerance that first causes and then exacerbates it.[4]

Ennis and Jack's love for each other does not correspond to socially acceptable emotions, and this engenders shame and the internalization of the socially dominant values. The late Heath Ledger, discussing the character that he so remarkably portrayed, stated: "Fear was instilled in him at an early age, and so the way he loved disgusted him."[5] In a remarkable acting performance, Ledger embodies this fear, self-repression, and self-loathing. Mendelsohn writes:

> The awkward, almost hobbled quality of his gait, the constricted gestures, the way in which he barely opens his mouth when he talks all speak eloquently of a man who is tormented simply by being in his own body—by being himself.[6]

Ennis swallows his words as he swallows his feelings.

CLOSETED LOVE

When Ennis visits Jack's childhood home toward the film's end, he discovers in his closet the shirts they wore on the last day of the summer they first met sheepherding on Brokeback Mountain. (Ennis thought he had lost his, but it turns out that Jack had stolen it as a keepsake.) Jack's shirt hugs his own on the same hanger. Mendelsohn writes:

> When Ennis sees them he is made aware too late of how greatly he was loved, of the extent of his loss. Ennis stands in the tiny windowless space caressing the shirts and weeping wordlessly.[7]

The last scene of the movie is shot in Ennis's trailer. He has reversed the shirts in his closet, placing Jack's blue within his own plaid shirt and pinned a tattered Brokeback Mountain postcard on the inside of the closet door. He straightens the card and carefully fastens the top button of Jack's shirt. Their two lives, like their shirts, have been closeted since the time they first met, two decades earlier.

With tears in his eyes, Ennis begins, "Jack, I swear," then closes the closet door and never finishes the sentence.[8] Owing to the fear and shame of homophobia and the dysphoria it induced in him, that cutoff sentence, an oath never finalized, symbolizes their truncated love.

NOTES

1. Annie Proulx, *Brokeback Mountain*. New York: Scribner, 1997, 15.
2. Ibid., 29.

3. Kenneth Turan, *Los Angeles Times*, quoted in Daniel Mendelsohn, "An Affair to Remember," *New York Review of Books*, 53:12–13 (Feb. 23, 2006).

4. Mendelsohn, ibid.

5. Ibid.

6. Ibid.

7. Ibid.

8. Proulx, 54.

Chapter Fourteen

A Shame-Inducing Epiphany in James Joyce's "The Dead"

An "epiphany" in literature is a sudden, powerful, and often life-changing insight into the reality or essential meaning of something, usually initiated by some ordinary, homely, or commonplace occurrence or experience.

"The Dead," a short story by James Joyce (1882–1941), is the last of the fifteen stories comprising Joyce's *Dubliners*, each of which contains an epiphany. "Epiphany" was used by Joyce as a secular term, although it initially referred to the Twelfth Night (January 6), when the Three Wise Men visited Christ, who revealed His divinity to them.

The concept of "epiphany" is explored from a Joycean perspective by Harry Levin, one of his biographers:

> Sometimes, amid the most encumbered circumstances, it suddenly happens that the veil is lifted, the burthen of the mystery laid bare, and the ultimate secret of things made manifest. . . . The task of the man of letters (according to Joyce) was to record these delicate and evanescent states of mind, to become a collector of epiphanies. . . . Listen for the single word that tells the whole story. Look for the simple gesture that reveals a complex set of relationships. It follows that the writer, like the mystic, must be particularly aware of these manifestations. What seem trivial details to others may be portentous symbols to him.[1]

Shame, defined as a painful feeling arising from the awareness of some dishonorable inadequacy, may derive from an archaic root *skam*, associated with clothing or the lack thereof.[2] Indeed, shame often arises when something concealed (notably the genitalia) is exposed. Mortifying shame (from the Latin root *mort-*, death) is so unbearable that death appears desirable. This is especially tragic because what has been exposed is often not horrific. In "The Dead," for example, mortifying shame arises in the

64

context of the protagonist's jealousy over his wife's deceased former lover, of whom he learns in the course of a Christmas party.

The protagonist of "The Dead," Gabriel Conroy, experiences four shame-inducing encounters during a Christmas Eve party. The presence of Christmas in the background of the story heightens the difference between Conroy and Michael Furey, his wife's former lover, in Conroy's mind. Having Christ in the air at the party makes of Furey a Christ-like figure that Gabriel (with his galoshes, as we shall see) can never match.

Conroy (who is perhaps Joyce's alter ego) is a university lecturer, a literary critic, and a thoughtful albeit egocentric man; his wife Gretta is a caring woman. The Conroys attend the annual Christmas party given by two maiden aunts, the Misses Morkan, and a fortyish-year-old cousin. There is much dancing, eating, and drinking, which sets the background for Gabriel's shame-induced encounters.

LILY: OPENING THE DOOR TO SHAME

Gabriel's first encounter with shame occurs soon after arriving at the party when greeted at the front door by Lily, the Morkans' servant, whom he has known from her childhood, when she would sit on the lower steps nursing a rag doll. He learns that she has finished school and jocularly inquires about her plans for marriage. She responds with unexpected candor and bitterness: "The men that is now is only all palaver and what they can get out of you."[3]

Gabriel blushes: "The high color of his cheeks pushed upwards even to his forehead where it scattered itself in a few formless patches of pale red."[4] His discomfort remains and "cast[s] a gloom over him which he tried to dispel."[5] Only later in the story, when we learn that Gabriel lusts after Gretta but has never loved her as Furey did, do we understand that Lily's accusatory sentence about her suitors strikes home: with respect to Gretta, he, too, is "only all palaver," and "what [he] can get out of [her]."

He tries to smooth matters over, trying to drop the subject by thrusting a coin into Lily's hands saying, "It's Christmas time, isn't it?" Lily refuses the "hush" money but Gabriel insists, waving his hand to her in deprecation.

Waiting outside the drawing room door for the waltz to end, listening to the skirts that sweep against it and the shuffling of feet, Gabriel remains "discomposed by the girl's bitter and sudden retort." He tries to dispel his mood by straightening his cuffs and tie, obsessing over the headings of the after-dinner speech he is to give, and assuming an air of superiority. Joyce writes, "The indelicate clacking of the men's heels and the shuffling of their soles reminded him that their grade of culture differed from his."

Nothing works to alleviate his anxiety. Gabriel fears "he would fail with [the guests] just as he had failed with the girl in the pantry. . . . His whole speech was a mistake from first to last." Forcing Christmas money on Lily instead of offering her the gift of self—sharing her pain—deprives them both of authentic contact, is depersonalizing, and contributes to his identity "fade-out," the denouement of the story.

GRETTA AND GABRIEL: CYCLES OF GUILT AND SHAME

A guilt-shame cycle at the party is set into motion by Gabriel, who deals with his embarrassment that he and his wife were late to the party by blaming Gretta: "My wife here takes three mortal hours to dress herself." Gretta gets even by deprecating Gabriel as father and husband, complaining to his aunts that he makes their son lift dumbbells, forces their daughter to eat "stirabout" (oatmeal porridge), which the daughter hates, and insists that Gretta wear galoshes. "The next thing he'll buy me," she teases, "will be a diving suit."[6] Gabriel laughs nervously at this and pats his tie reassuringly.

Despite their superficial banter, Gretta is pained—her husband is insensitive to her needs and those of their children. By disregarding her complaints and distancing himself from shame by blaming, he perpetuates a guilt-shame cycle, not uncommon in emotionally "stormy" relationships.

MOLLY IVORS: "EATING CROW"

As guests at the party assemble for a square dance, Molly Ivors, Gabriel's long-standing friend and colleague, announces she has a "crow to pluck" with him. She asks him who "G.C." is, which causes him to blush, and says, "I have found out that you write for *The Daily Express*. Now, aren't you ashamed of yourself?"[7]

She upbraids him for his literary column in this conservative paper, which opposes home rule: "Well, I'm ashamed of you. . . . To say you'd write for a paper like that. I didn't think you were a West Briton!"[8] Gabriel wants to say that literature is above politics but only murmurs lamely that he sees nothing political in writing book reviews.

Molly questions Gabriel's patriotism, and the other guests turn to listen to her cross-examination, which makes "a blush invade his forehead."[9] Gabriel tries to regain composure by throwing himself into a quadrille with great energy, avoiding eye contact with Molly, retreating to a far corner of the room, and striking up a conversation with an old friend; but he cannot distract his mind from the unpleasant episode, and ponders the matter: "She had no right to call him a West Briton in front of people, even in joke. She had tried to make him ridiculous before people, heckling him and staring at him with her rabbit's eyes."[10] He longs to flee:

> How cool it must be outside! How pleasant it would be to walk out alone, first along by the river and then through the park! . . . How much more pleasant it would be there than at the supper-table![11]

Molly has touched a raw nerve. Gabriel has mixed feelings about participating in the home-rule movement but does not acknowledge them, even to himself. Instead, he argues with her about the absence of politics in his book review and tries to justify the review ("literature above politics"), but neither strategy refutes her point.

Because Gabriel is not forthcoming about his ambivalence in writing for the pro-Anglo "rag," he is unable "to banish from his mind all memory of the unpleasant incident," and his thinking takes a paranoid turn: "Perhaps she would not be sorry to see him fail in his speech."[12]

GRETTA, GABRIEL, AND THE TRIANGULAR RELATIONSHIP WITH A DEAD MAN

During Bartell D'Arcy's rendition of the poignant ballad "The Lass of Aughrim," Gretta vividly recollects Michael Furey, a delicate youth with a tenor voice who literally died over his love for her. He had sung the same heartbreaking piece. The story began when she was living in Galway (in western Ireland) and decided to enter a convent.

Aware that Furey was ill and wouldn't be allowed to see her off, she wrote him saying she would be back in the summer and hoped he would be better by then. On the eve of her departure Furey appeared in the rain beneath a tree nearby her lodgings. Gretta realized he was jeopardizing his health by being out in such weather, but Furey said he didn't want to live without her. A week after entering the convent, Gretta learned that he had died.

Gabriel comes to realize that "while he had been full of memories of their secret life together, full of tenderness and joy and desire [Gretta] had been comparing him in her mind with another." Gabriel's humiliation is overwhelming:

> A shameful consciousness of his own person assailed him. He saw himself as a ludicrous figure, acting as a pennyboy for his aunts, a nervous, well-meaning

sentimentalist, orating to vulgarians and idealising his own clownish lusts, the pitiable fatuous fellow he had caught a glimpse of in the mirror.[13]

Gretta has her own emotional problems, which stir up her husband's. Although Furey has been dead many years, she is consumed by grief while describing his death: "She stopped, choking with sobs, and, overcome by emotion, flung herself face downward on the bed, sobbing in the quilt."[14]

She relives the traumatic event, symptomatic of those with post-traumatic stress disorder (PTSD): "I can see him so plainly. . . . Such eyes as he had: big, dark eyes! And such an expression in the eyes. . . . I implored of him to go home at once and told him he would get his death in the rain. But he said he did not want to live. I can see his eyes as well as well!"[15] Her psychic numbing, another symptom of PTSD, may account for the lack of intimacy between the Conroys. Gabriel ponders "how poor a part he, her husband, had played in her life."[16]

Undoubtedly, Gretta is plagued by guilt. Although Furey said he did not want to live if she entered a convent, she departed anyway and then learned he had died. Guilt may complicate grief-work, and Gretta's choking sobs suggest incompletely expressed grief. Thus, Gretta's contribution to the marital impasse includes grief, guilt, and PTSD.

Gabriel Conroy is this story's protagonist, and Joyce's artistry is to show, through the evening's sequence of events, how they culminate in an epiphany that induces mortifying shame.

Joyce said he had not read Chekhov's stories when he was writing his own.[17] Yet a number of parallels exist between "The Dead" and Chekhov's "Lady with the Pet Dog"—the story to which we now turn, which involves not one but two triangular relationships.

NOTES

1. Harry Levin, *James Joyce: A Critical Introduction*, New York: New Directions, 1960, 28–29.

2. Cf. Anatoly Liberman, "Guilt Societies and Shame Societies, or, Shame and Guilt from an Etymological Point of View," *Oxford Etymologist,* Sept. 3, 2008, http://blog.oup.com/2008/09/guilt_shame/ —Accessed Mar. 26, 2009.

3. James Joyce, "The Dead," in *Dubliners* (New York: Random House, 1954), 227.

4. Ibid., 228.

5. Ibid., 229.

6. Ibid., 231.

7. Ibid., 240.

8. Ibid., 240–41.
9. Ibid., 248.
10. Ibid., 244.
11. Ibid., 246.
12. Ibid.
13. Ibid., 283.
14. Ibid., 285.
15. Ibid., 282, 284.
16. Ibid., 285.
17. Richard Ellman, *James Joyce* (Oxford: Oxford University Press, 1982), 166n.

Chapter Fifteen

Chekhov's "Lady with the Pet Dog": A Womanizer Learns to Love

Anton Chekhov—like James Joyce—made extensive use of epiphany in his stories, and both his "Lady with the Pet Dog" and Joyce's "The Dead" use that literary device to unfold their theme of mortifying shame. Each story deals with a protagonist who unexpectedly becomes involved in a romantic triangle. The differing responses of the two couples (Anna Sergeyevna and Dmitry Gurov in "Lady with the Pet Dog," and Gretta and Gabriel Conroy in "The Dead") cast light on the nature of their relationships and on the psychology of shame.

"Lady with the Pet Dog," (sometimes translated as "The Lady with the Lapdog") relates the story of a forty-year-old womanizer, Dmitry Gurov, a Moscow banker and an unhappily married father of three, who has an affair with a young woman, Anna Sergeyevna, also unhappily married. The affair begins while both are vacationing in Yalta, a chic Crimean seaside resort known for trysts. Their love does not rescue them from their bad marriages, however, and Chekhov doesn't provide a solution to their plight. He does, however, insightfully depict their shame. As Maxim Gorky commented:

> No one understood as clearly and finely as Anton Chekhov, the tragedy of life's trivialities, no one before him showed men with such merciless truth the terrible and shameful picture of their life in the dim chaos of bourgeois every-day existence.[1]

The first encounter of these ill-starred lovers results from an interchange between Gurov and the young lady's dog:

> He beckoned invitingly to the Pomeranian and, when the dog approached him, shook his finger at it. The Pomeranian growled; Gurov threatened it again. The

lady glanced at him and instantly lowered her eyes. "He doesn't bite," she said and blushed.[2]

In this vignette, a microcosmic view of their relationship, we observe that Gurov is a seductive, rejecting manipulator and that Anna is easily shamed. This dynamic is evident after they have become physically intimate. Gurov swallows slices of watermelon and spits out the seeds while Anna excoriates herself. "It's not right. You don't respect me now. God forgive me!" she exclaims, and her eyes fill up with tears. "I am a bad, low woman; I despise myself."

Anna had married at twenty, discovered she wanted something more than "a flunkey" for a husband, and tried to control her passions but could not. She has told her husband that she is ill and has left for the spa at Yalta, where she has encountered Gurov.

Gurov is a philanderer and becomes annoyed at her self-deprecation, which is unanticipated and inappropriate in his estimation. When she cuts short her vacation to return home because her husband has an eye infection, he ends the affair in his mind: "There had now been another episode or adventure in his life and it, too, was at an end, and nothing was left of it but a memory."[3]

Back in Moscow, however, Gurov is unable to erase Anna from his mind:

> Of evenings she peered out at him from the bookcase, from the fireplace, from the corner—he heard her breathing, the caressing rustle of her clothes. In the street he followed the women with his eyes, looking for someone who resembled her. . . . Anna Sergeyevna did not [merely] come to him in his dreams, she accompanied him everywhere, like his shadow, following him everywhere he went.[4]

Fed up with his wife and children, as well as with his job at the bank, Gurov sets off to the provinces to see Anna—a new response for this connoisseur specialist in one-night stands.

They begin an adulterous relationship behind closed doors in the provinces where she lives and in a Moscow hotel where Anna visits him. There, at a rendezvous, he catches a glimpse of himself in a mirror and notes how "[h]is hair was already beginning to turn gray. And it seemed odd to him that he had grown so much older in the last few years, and lost his looks."[5]

Although he has aged, this womanizer is in the process of a rebirth. When Anna weeps over their plight, his responses are now quite supportive:

> Formerly in moments of sadness he had soothed himself with whatever logical arguments came into his head, but now he no longer cared for logic; he felt profound compassion, he wanted to be sincere and tender:

"Give it up now, my darling," he said. "You've had your cry; that's enough. Let us have a talk now, we'll think up something." Then they spent a long time taking counsel together.[6]

MORTIFICATION IN "THE DEAD" AND TRANSFORMATION IN "LADY WITH THE PET DOG"

When we compare Chekhov's tale with Joyce's, the contrast is evident. Gabriel Conroy's ultimate response to the onslaughts of shame is ambiguous. In the concluding passage of "The Dead," Joyce writes: "The time had come for him to set out on his journey westward."[7] Since the west is the traditional locale of death, and Gabriel becomes conscious of the "wayward and flickering existence" of the dead, it is safe to assume that the westward journey is, at least in part, the journey toward death.

But westward also pertains to the western region of Ireland, former habitat of Gretta and of Michael Furey, and lodestone of Molly Ivors; a rural domain whose down-to-earth values of simplicity, hospitality, passion, and compassion Gabriel is tempted to embrace. Death and the passionate life are both in Gabriel's mind as he lies down alongside his wife and ruminates: "Better pass boldly in that other world, in the full glory of some passion, than fade and wither dismally with age."[8]

The object of Gabriel's passion is Gretta, but the possibilities of a passionate relationship with her are slim because instead of sharing his feelings of shame with her, "instinctively he turned his back more to the light lest she might see the shame that burned upon his forehead."[9] He decides not to question her further about Furey, "for he felt that she would tell him of herself."[10] Gretta's hand, though warm and moist, does not respond to his touch.

Gabriel, feeling ashamed and depersonalized, undergoes psychological death. He swoons into a hypnagogic state of consciousness and, mortified by shame, "approached that region where dwell the vast hosts of the dead." [11]

In contrast, Anna and Gurov

> forgave each other what they were ashamed of in their past, they forgave everything in the present, and felt that this love of theirs had altered them both. . .
>
> And it seemed as though in a little while the solution would be found, and then a new and glorious life would begin; and it was clear to both of them that the end was still far off, and that what was to be most complicated and difficult for them was only just beginning.[12]

Love has gradually transformed Gurov, a habitual lecher, from cynical to respectful. He stands patiently while Anna sits, and he no longer looks over her shoulder while kissing her; but the story, like "The Dead," ends abruptly in *medias res*, without offering a facile solution to the protagonists' complex marital problems.

NOTES

1. Maxim Gorky, *Reminiscences of Anton Chekhov*, tr. S. S. Koteliansky and Leonard Woolf. New York: B. W. Huebsch, 1921. Reprinted at http://www.ibiblio .org/eldritch/ac/gorky.htm — Accessed Mar. 31, 2008.

2. Anton Chekhov, *The Portable Chekhov*, 414.

3. Ibid., 421.

4. Ibid., 423–24.

5. Ibid., 432.

6. Ibid., 433.

7. Joyce, "The Dead," 287.

8. Ibid.

9. Ibid., 283.

10. Ibid., 284.

11. Ibid., 287.

12. *Portable Chekhov*, 433.

Chapter Sixteen

Joseph Conrad's *Lord Jim*: Inner and Outer Courts of Inquiry

"THE ACUTE CONSCIOUSNESS OF LOST HONOR"

Joseph Conrad (1857–1924), author of the novel *Lord Jim* (1900), saw his story as a "free and wandering tale [about] the acute consciousness of lost honor."[1]

With the opening words of the novel, readers become aware that Jim has shortcomings: "He was an inch, perhaps two, under six feet." Although "powerfully, built," "spotlessly neat," and "appareled in immaculate white from shoes to hat," he advances "with a slight stoop of the shoulders."[2]

Conrad's protagonist presents himself to others with the stature, attire, and posture of a man conscious of lost honor, honor lost because of a tragic psychological flaw: under stress, Jim's thinking is not straight and clear, involving him in poorly planned, or unplanned, actions he later regrets.

Jim also has heroic dreams of glory, which create an enormous gap between what he would like to do and what he actually does when stressed. This gap evokes "the acute consciousness of lost honor."

The heroic strivings are evident from Jim's fantasies:

He saw himself saving people from sinking ships, cutting away masts in a hurricane, swimming through a surf with a line. . . . He confronted savages on tropical shores, quelled mutinies on the high seas, and in a small boat upon the ocean kept up the hearts of despairing men—always an example of devotion to duty, and as unflinching as a hero in a book.[3]

Jim's aspirations were undoubtedly instilled in him by his father, a parson who

[p]ossessed such certain knowledge of the Unknowable as made for the righteousness of people in cottages without disturbing the ease of mind of those whom an unerring Providence enables to live in mansions.[4]

The first of the two major stressors in Jim's life occurs when he is a young first mate on the *Patna*, a merchant boat carrying eight hundred Arab pilgrims to Mecca for a hajj. The ship hits a submerged object and springs a leak; there is an upcoming storm and Jim impulsively abandons ship. At a later date, another character reconstructs how Jim must have reacted:

> Shock slight. . . . Stopped the ship. Ascertained the damage. Took measures to get the boats out without creating a panic. As the first boat was lowered ship went down in a squall. Sank like lead. . . . I had jumped, hadn't I . . . That's what I had to live down. The story didn't matter.[5]

In fact, the *Patna* does not sink, although given the press of events it seemed that way. A maritime Court of Inquiry finds that Jim and the crew acted "in utter disregard of . . . plain duty abandoning in the moment of danger the lives and property confided to their charge."[6] Thus—because of Jim's stress disorder—his seaman's certificate is revoked.

Captain Marlow, a sympathetic and experienced seaman who narrates the first part of the novel, meets Jim at the inquiry and identifies with him, insisting that Jim is "one of us." In time, Marlow becomes aware that his friend travels incognito, working from port to port, until his identity is exposed (or is in danger of being revealed) then drifts on.

"In the Destructive Element Immerse"

Marlow, in an attempt to help his friend in some way, decides to discuss Jim's life of flight with Stein, a learned colleague, much as these days one might arrange a consultation with a good psychoanalyst. After hearing the saga of the humiliated man, Stein, a merchant whose avocation is entomology, compares Jim to one of his beloved butterflies:

> This magnificent butterfly finds a little heap of dirt and sits still on it; but man can never on his little heap of mud sit still. He wants to be so, and again he wants to be so.[7]

Speaking in a style reminiscent of a Viennese Freudian and giving good psychoanalytic advice, Stein draws a parallel between Jim and a novice swimmer:

A man that is born falls into a dream like a man who falls into the sea. If he tries to climb out into the air as inexperienced people endeavor to do, he drowns—*nicht wahr?* . . . No! I tell you! The way is to the destructive element submit yourself, and with the exertions of your hands and feet in the water make the deep, deep sea keep you up. . . . In the destructive element immerse.[8]

The "destructive element," shame, erodes the psyche unless its source is identified and transcended. Jim's shame stems from his stress disorder, which became a judicial issue, then a moral issue—he feels that by jumping, he did something "bad."

With the stress of an oncoming storm, a leak in the ship, and the calls of the ship's captain to jump, Jim failed to process the ethical and legal implications of his actions. Running away from shame, however, prevents him from understanding his particular vulnerability to stress. He has not submitted himself to the "destructive element"—Stein's prescription.

Stein offers to make Jim his agent on a Malaysian island, Patusan, where there is very little danger that his identity will be uncovered. Only two letters (*us*) distinguish Patna from Patusan, so one may surmise that the second part of Jim's "wandering tale [about] the acute consciousness of lost honor" will not differ much from the first.

Patusan and the Repetition Compulsion

Jim conducts himself admirably on Patusan until, once again, he is overwhelmed by stress and his thinking is impaired. As a consequence, he presents himself to the father of a man whose son dies because of another of his stress-related errors of judgment, and asks for a release from the mortifying shame, saying, "Time to finish this." The grieving father kills Jim with a gunshot wound to the heart. It is as if he (or his biological father) had pulled the trigger to punish him for his two episodes of "shameful" conduct.

Lord Jim, with its multiple perspectives on Jim (Marlow's narratives often bring in other characters who differ on their take of this flawed hero) lays the foundation for such modern novels as William Faulkner's *The Sound and the Fury*, with its kaleidoscopic narrative complexities.

Stein's admonition, "In the destructive element immerse," is psychologically sophisticated. Without recognizing and dealing with his stress disorder, Jim "attempted to climb out into the air" by going to Malaysia. Unfortunately, the "repetition compulsion" pursued him.

NOTES

1. Joseph Conrad, "Author's Note" [1917], *Lord Jim*, Thomas C. Moser, ed. (New York: Norton, 1996), 5–6.

2. Conrad, *Lord Jim*, 7.

3. Ibid., 9.

4. Ibid., 8.

5. Ibid., 82.

6. Ibid., 97.

7. Ibid., 128–29.

8. Ibid., 129–30.

Chapter Seventeen

Edward Hopper's Last Painting, *Two Comedians*: An Ego-Absolving Gloss

"Great art," Edward Hopper (1882–1967) wrote, "is the outward expression of an inner life in the artist. . . . The man's the work. Something does not come out of nothing."[1] Fellow artist and compatriot Charles Burchfield concurred: "With Hopper, the whole fabric of his art seems to be interwoven with his personal character and manner of living."[2]

The outward expressions of Hopper's inner life are the eerie, melancholic, enigmatic, and realistic depictions of the solitude and loneliness of life in America. His choice of subjects—a deserted Gloucester street, the back rows of a New York City movie house, a desolate gas station opposite a foreboding woodland scene, train tracks coming from someplace and going to who knows where—convey a stark rural or depersonalized urban scene in the United States. The harsh light permeating his scene may be contrasted with the softer glow of Norman Rockwell's images from the same epoch—his *Thanksgiving Day* depiction of *gemütlichkeit* around the dinner table, or *Home from a Family Vacation*. Rockwell presents different views of life in the U.S.A. in warm luminescence.

Although Hopper was inseparable from his wife, Josephine (Jo) Nivison, for more than forty years, apparently they had a tumultuous love-hate relationship. Biographer Gail Levin, drawing from Josephine's diary, contends that their "acute anguish in personal life transmuted into [his] gripping art. . . . Their pictorial idiom, at once familiar and estranged, touches our memories, hopes, uncertainties—the yearning and disquiet of modern lives."[3]

"Ed," Josephine confided in her lengthy diary, "is the very centre of my universe [but] if he sees I'm on the point of being very happy, he sees to it that I'm not." She depicts her husband as an introverted, sexually repressed misogynist who ridiculed, degraded, and thwarted her artistic career. Talking with him "was like taking the attention of an expensive specialist. . . . He would often look at his watch."

Hopper was aware that he put art above personal relations: "Maybe I am slightly inhuman. . . . All I ever wanted to do was to paint sunlight on the side of a house." It appears he had a melancholic temperament and that his physician prescribed Benzedrine for "depression, fatigue and lethargy."[4]

It may be that Hopper's capacity for social relationships was impaired, similar to those with Asperger disorder, and he depicted the state of emotional detachment in many of his paintings, for example, in the loneliness of the *Automat* (1927). Josephine, a gregarious person, full of energy, at times broke through his disconnected state.

Hopper's last painting, *Two Comedians* (1965), portrays the artist and his wife as Pierrot and Columbine in commedia dell'arte costumes, holding hands and bowing, taking the final applause. The painting is described in this poem, which I wrote based on Levin's book:

> Jo and Ed
>
> Hopper's last oil—
> A marriage biopic—
> Turned the spot
> On him and Jo
> In one image:
>
> "Two Comedians"
> (Pierrot & Columbine)
> Holding hands & bowing,
> Sharing the limelight
> And final applause.
>
> But Ed shoved Jo
> Into the wings
> Whenever he could,
> And she kept trying
> To upstage him:
>
> "Why fuss so over Ed?
> I am just as good as he,"
> She told a dealer
> Two years before Ed's death,
> When he was in Art's pantheon.

Not "Two Comedians,"
An ego-absolving gloss,
But Grant Wood's *American Gothic*,
Although generic,
Conveys their quintessence:

Lover-enemies.
He comes first as usual,
Jaw set, rigid pitchfork in fist.
She's close behind,
Wearing reform collar,
Prim, fuming, mortified.[5]

Hopper died two years after painting *Two Comedians*. Following his death, Josephine wrote a friend that their forty-two years together had reached a "perfection (of its own snappy kind)." Apparently, Josephine was able to transcend her mortifying shame.

NOTES

1. Quoted in Edward Lucie-Smith, *Lives of the Great 20th-Century Artists*. London: Thames & Hudson, 1999, ch. 16.
2. Ibid.
3. Gail Levin, *Edward Hopper: An Intimate Biography*. New York: Knopf, 1995, xvii
4. Ibid., 305.
5. Michael Sperber, "Jo & Ed," *Provincetown Arts*, 1997, 110.

Chapter Eighteen

Alexander Pushkin's "The Shot": Revenge, a Dish Best Savored Cold

It is possible to cope with mortifying shame without retaliation or sinking into profound despair. Alexander Pushkin (1799–1837), who is often considered the founder of contemporary Russian literature, presents an account of one way to accomplish this in his short story "The Shot" (1830).

The protagonist of the tale, Silvio, is humiliated by a man for whom he consequently feels murderous envy. With patience and perseverance, Silvio rectifies matters in such a way that nobody is hurt. In the process, he learns about the nature of jealousy, which enhances his feelings of self-worth.

Silvio, a thirty-five year old former military officer, is a man of mystery. Nobody knows why he resigned his commission or settled in a "wretched town," where "he lived poorly and, at the same time, extravagantly."[1] He always goes around on foot and wears a shabby coat, but provides dinners, amid flowing champagne, to which all the officers of the village are invited, and lends good books from his collection without asking for them back.

Silvio's main preoccupation is pistol-shooting. He practices target-shooting daily and the walls of his room are riddled with bullet holes. He possesses an extensive collection of firearms and is a formidable marksman. "If he had offered to shoot a pear off somebody's forage-cap," the narrator relates, "not a man in our regiment would have hesitated to expose his head to the bullet."[2]

The officers who visit him conclude that Silvio must have some victim of his incredible skill on his conscience. They do not suspect him of cowardice. One evening after the other guests leave, Silvio shares his story with the narrator: "Six years ago I received a slap in the face, and my enemy still lives," he says. "I did fight with him, and here is a souvenir of our duel."[3] He puts on an embroidered red cap with a gold tassel, which a bullet has penetrated about two inches above the forehead.

Once a passionate, riotous youth, worshipped by his comrades, Silvio was enjoying his reputation when a rich young man from a distinguished family joined the regiment. "Never before," Silvio continues, "ha[d] I met anyone so blessed or so brilliant . . . youth, intelligence, good looks, boundless gaiety, reckless courage, a great name, an inexhaustible supply of money."[4] Silvio's feelings of supremacy among his fellows are shaken.

The young man is attracted to him by his reputation, but Silvio treats him coldly. At a ball attended by a woman with whom Silvio is having an affair, the young man becomes the object of her attention, Silvio can no longer contain himself. He approaches and whispers some vulgarity in his ear, whereupon the youth slaps Silvio in the face. They arrange a duel.

The young man arrives at the designated site holding a hat in his hands filled with cherries. Silvio, supposed to shoot first, is so incensed that he is unable to rely on a steady hand and yields the first shot to his opponent, who doesn't accept it. They cast lots and the youth gets the first shot. He takes aim and the bullet passes through Silvio's hat.

Next, it is Silvio's turn and he scrutinizes his opponent, trying to detect in him the faintest sign of apprehension, but the latter stands in pistol range, culling ripe cherries from his cap and spitting out the pits so they land near Silvio's feet. The youth's composure in the face of death is provocative, and Silvio is jealous and provoked. If he places so little importance on life, what would be the value of depriving him of it? A malicious thought flashes through Silvio's mind, and he decides to defer his shot: "You don't seem to be ready for death just at present," he says, "You wish to have your breakfast; I do not wish to hinder you." The other replies: "Have the goodness to fire, or just as you please—you owe me a shot; I shall always be at your service."[5]

Silvio defers his shot, subsequently resigns his commission, and retires to the small town where we meet him at the start of the story, but not a day goes by that he does not think of getting revenge. Finally, the hour draws near. Silvio learns from an informant that his adversary has become engaged to a young and beautiful girl, and he muses: "We shall see if he will look death in the face with as much indifference now, when he is on the eve of being married, as he did once when he was eating cherries!"[6]

Several years later, the narrator is invited to the home of a wealthy count with a young and beautiful wife. While talking with his hosts, he notices a picture with two bullet holes in it, one directly above the other, and remarks that it must have been made by an expert marksman. The count states that it is a souvenir of the last meeting he had with a man who indeed had excellent aim, and he relates the encounter.

At the time of his marriage five years before, he was on his honeymoon when a visitor appeared. It was Silvio, who had come for his shot, but offered to cast lots to see who would shoot first. The count won and shot, but hit the picture.

Just as Silvio readies himself for his shot, the count's wife appears. Her husband evidences alarm and confusion. With that, Silvio saw what he came to see and, departing, glances at the picture through which the count's bullet passed. He shoots at it almost without aiming, and departs.

The story validates an old aphorism: "Revenge is a dish best eaten cold." Silvio, jealous of the youth's equanimity in the face of death, discovers that his adversary was not displaying bravery at the time of the first duel, only indifference to life. This observation enabled Silvio to overcome the jealousy and envy plaguing him for several years. Because he has resisted the temptation to act impulsively (unlike Conrad's Lord Jim), Silvio's insight into himself and others is enhanced.

Ironically, whereas Silvio avoids a duel, lives on, and learns and matures as a result, Pushkin was unable to do the same. He challenged Baron Georges d'Anthes to a duel after widespread gossip reached him that the latter was having an affair with his young, beautiful, frivolous wife, Natalya.

Pushkin is said to have received an anonymous note informing him that he had been elected to "The International Order of Cuckolds." Intellectual awareness does not always preclude unwise behaviors. "The Shot" describes a moral equivalent to revenge, but its author, unable to embody Silvio's self-restraint, died from peritonitis at the age of thirty-seven following a gunshot wound sustained in a duel with the baron.

NOTES

1. Avram Yarmolinksy, ed., *The Poems, Prose and Plays of Alexander Pushkin,* New York, Random House, 1936, 472.

2. Ibid., 473.

3. Ibid., 478.

4. Ibid.

5. Ibid., 480.

6. Ibid.

Part II

POST-TRAUMATIC STRESS DISORDER

Chapter Nineteen

Introduction:
The Many Facets of PTSD

Post-traumatic stress disorder (PTSD) is the term for severe and ongoing re-actions to a terrifying event or ordeal in which grave physical or psychologi-cal harm occurred or was threatened. A person's usual psychological defenses are unable to cope with the trauma, and a triad of characteristic symptoms occurs owing to incomplete processing of the trauma:

1. Intrusive symptoms: These include recurrent nightmares, daydreams, and flashbacks in which the trauma is reexperienced.
2. Hyperarousal: This refers to the state of hypervigilance that occurs in-volving a "flight or fight" response, and jumpiness in connection to loud sounds, vivid sights, or smells that trigger the initial trauma.
3. Avoidance: The intrusive and hyperarousal symptoms may be so dis-tressing that persons become detached and strive to avoid contact with everyone and everything—even their own thoughts—that may arouse memories of the trauma. Isolation occurs and a restriction of emotional responses is seen, called "psychic numbing" or "emotional anesthesia." Dissociation, depersonalization, and derealization may create distance from the shocking trauma. The sufferer then comes to feel he or she is "in another world."

The experiences that may induce this condition include childhood physi-cal, emotional, or sexual abuse or neglect; a serious accident; medical crises; assault or rape; the horrors of war; and violent or life-threatening natural disasters. Nathaniel Hawthorne undoubtedly developed PTSD when he was four years old, at the time his father, a ship's captain, failed to return home after developing yellow fever and dying on a voyage to Sumatra. Years later, young man Hawthorne wrote his way out of the mental jail in which he had been subsequently imprisoned. Frederick Law Olmsted, who stumbled on the scene of his mother dying from an overdose of laudanum, evolved the practice of landscape psychoarchitecture to help him cope with chronic PTSD. Both Alger Hiss and his fictional counterpart, Tolstoy's Aksenov, suffered from PTSD after being convicted and imprisoned for crimes of which they were innocent. Fortunately, both found ways to use the shocking experience, which ultimately contributed to their mental and spiritual growth.

Chapter Twenty

Nathaniel Hawthorne's "Wakefield": Sleepwalker in a Mental Jail

The behavior of the eponymous antihero of the Kafkaesque "Wakefield," a short story by Nathaniel Hawthorne (1804–1864), is quite bizarre on a conscious level. Hawthorne acknowledged that Wakefield was "as remarkable a freak as may be found in the whole list of human oddities." The narrator provides evidence:

> The man, under pretence of going a journey, took lodgings in the next street to his own house, and there, unheard of by his wife or friends, and without the shadow of a reason for such self-banishment, dwelt upwards of twenty years. During that period, he beheld his home every day and frequently the forlorn Mrs. Wakefield. After so great a gap in marital felicity—when his death was reckoned certain . . . he entered the door one evening, quietly, as from a day's absence, and became a loving spouse till death.[1]

The words in this paragraph make more sense with a bracketed insertion: "without the shadow of a [conscious] reason for such self-banishment." In this section, we explore some of the unconscious determinants in Hawthorne's trauma-ridden childhood, using insights derived from Carl Jung's Trickster archetype to understand it better.

"WAKEFIELD": A WAKE-UP CALL TO A HALF-AWAKE WAKEFIELD

Hawthorne's choice of names provides a clue to understanding his bizarre protagonist. Wakefield is sleepwalking through life and needs to awaken. He has been asleep in a field where he should have been working. The narrator relates that

> a certain sluggishness would keep his heart at rest, wherever it might be placed. He was intellectual, but not actively so; his mind occupied itself in long and lazy musings, that tended to no purpose, or had not vigor to attain it, his thoughts were seldom so energetic as to seize hold of words. . . . A quiet selfishness . . . had rusted into his inactive mind.[2]

Wakefield could be described as a sleepwalker in a mental dungeon, of which Hawthorne wrote to his classmate Henry Wadsworth Longfellow, as discussed below.

A Mental Dungeon

After the death of Nathaniel Hawthorne's father, Captain Nathaniel Hathorne (1775–1808), Hawthorne's early years were unremarkable except for a foot injury that confined him to quarters for some two years when he was a youngster, which gave him an opportunity to read and read. It also may have made it difficult to "step out" years later. He attended school in Salem, Massachusetts, went to Bowdoin College in Maine, graduated in 1825, and returned to his room in Salem, the "little chamber under the eves" where he remained the next dozen years, vacating his life as did Wakefield, an alter ego. Hawthorne described the room as a mental "dungeon" in a letter to fellow Bowdoin alumnus Henry Wadsworth Longfellow.

> By some witchcraft or other—for I really cannot assign any reasonable why and wherefore—I have been carried apart from the main current of life, and find it impossible to get back again. . . . I have secluded myself from society; and yet I never meant any such thing, nor dreamed what sort of life I was going to lead. I have made a captive of myself and put me into a dungeon; and now I cannot find the key to let myself out—and if the door were open, I should be almost afraid to come out.[3]

The younger Hawthorne added the "*w*" to his surname while in college, possibly to distance himself from a tyrannical ancestor, Judge John Hathorne (1641–1717), who achieved notoriety in the Salem witchcraft trials with his harsh dispensation of "justice." There was a family legend that one of his victims placed a curse on the judge and his descendants before she was hanged.[4] Perhaps Hawthorne also wanted to distance himself from his sea-captain father, whom he may have imagined as a mischievous trickster, as we shall see.

He found the key in composing some forty stories in which he explored many of the psychological issues with which he himself had been grappling. The role of father-husband, chief among them, is central to such masterpieces as "Roger Malvin's Burial" (1831), "The Gentle Boy" (1831), "Young Goodman Brown" (1835), and "Wakefield" (1836).

Since "Wakefield" was one of the last stories Hawthorne wrote before exiting from the "dungeon," one may assume that it contains important clues about the psyche of its enigmatic antihero and insight into the author's mental jail.

Oedipal Guilt and a "Crafty Nincompoop"

Four-year-old Nathaniel must have been overwhelmed by guilt following his father's "disappearance" and his mother's reclusive withdrawal. He coped with the ensuing post-traumatic stress syndrome using denial, which is evidenced in "Wakefield." In that narrative he seems to say, "Father isn't really dead, but just moved up the next street and will return someday, like the 'crafty nincompoop,' [his term for Wakefield] after his long 'whim-wham.' I did not kill him and mother will not abandon me in grief and rage."

Wakefield has a characteristic facial expression that illuminates his personality. Mrs. Wakefield glimpses it when her husband says good-bye. He closes the door, then thrusts it open, and she envisions his face smiling at her. That smile recurs to her even a decade later and her death wish is clear: "She imagines him in a coffin, that parting look is frozen on his pale features. Still his blessed spirit wears a quiet and *crafty* smile."[5] (Emphasis added.)

Hawthorne calls Wakefield a "*crafty* nincompoop," and refers to his *crafty* disposition. This personality characteristic is evident even twenty years later, when he finally returns home:

> The door opens. As he passes in, again we have a parting glimpse of his visage and recognize the *crafty* smile, which was the precursor of the little joke that he was playing off at his wife's expense.[6] (Emphasis added.)

This twenty-year-old "little joke" well qualifies Wakefield for the Jungian archetypical designation "Trickster." Hawthorne writes, "His harmless love of mystery . . . almost resolved to perplex his good lady."[7]

SHADOW AND TRICKSTER

Carl Jung noted: "Who looks outside dreams. Who looks inside awakes." Crafty Wakefield never looked within and never awakes until the story's end.

The etymology of "crafty" is illuminating. In Old English, *craeftig* meant "strong," "skillful." Hawthorne most likely felt abandoned at an early age by a father he considered "crafty," who would someday return home. It would seem that crafty Wakefield used the skill and strength of the Trickster within, at least in an attempt to wake up.

The goal of life according to Jung is to individuate—to be who we are, without mask or pretense. *Personality* has as its root the Latin *persona,* a "mask." An authentic self resides beneath the mask of personality, and the Trickster expedites the journey of self-recovery.

Although Wakefield tells his wife he is taking "the night coach into the country," he does not take a geographic journey. His pilgrimage is to the dark side of his psyche and he vacates his life, it could be said, to get a better view of it. A middle-aged man ten years into a marriage, he is in a midlife crisis and on some level must feel a lack of meaning in his life.

On the thinking/feeling axis, Wakefield is out of touch with his feelings, more an observer than a participant, with a "cold, but not depraved or wandering heart."[8] Unencumbered by feelings, however, he is sharp-eyed. In the third week of absence from home, for example, he overlooks nothing pertaining to Mrs. Wakefield and gradually his feelings begin to return:

> Twice or thrice has she passed before his sight, each time with a heavier step, a paler cheek, and more anxious brow; . . . he detects a portent of evil entering the house, in the guise of an apothecary. Next day, the knocker is muffled. . . . Dear woman! Will she die? By this time, Wakefield *is excited to something like energy of feeling.*[9]

Tricksters: Like Father, Like Son

"What sort of a man was Wakefield?" the author rhetorically asks at the onset of his perplexing tale. "We are free to shape our own idea, and call it by his name," he writes.[10] What determined Hawthorne's perceptions of the personality of Wakefield, who left home as mysteriously and abruptly as his own father? Most likely they were shaped by Hawthorne's projections, and there is evidence that the author, like his antihero, was himself something of a Trickster. Like father like son: Julian, the middle of Nathaniel Hawthorne's three offspring, was also a Trickster, for which he spent time in prison, as we shall see.

Nathaniel Hawthorne met Elizabeth Peabody in 1837 (the year "Wakefield" was published) before encountering her sister, Sophia, whom he married in 1842. Elizabeth was apparently smitten by him, referring to Hawthorne as "one of Nature's ordained priests." When she asked if he considered it "healthy to live so separated" as he had been, alone in his attic chamber, he admitted, "It is the misfortune of my life. It has produced a morbid consciousness that paralyses my powers."[11]

Elizabeth engaged in public relations on Hawthorne's behalf, promoting his work, perhaps trying to win him over. She reviewed his *Twice-Told Tales*, describing it as a "little book of caged melodies," predicting the author's "place amongst the contemporaries as the greatest artist of his line" since he "displayed so great a variety of the elements of genius."[12]

Because Hawthorne made no effort to dissuade Elizabeth from furthering his literary career, she sent a copy of *Twice-Told Tales* to Horace Mann, an education reformer, suggesting that he use its author to write stories for children. According to one biographer, "Elizabeth allowed Nathaniel Hawthorne to become more than just a genius to promote. She fell in love—with the man, with his stories, even with his eccentric family. And . . . Nathaniel Hawthorne let Elizabeth believe—may have believed himself—that he loved her back."[13]

The attachment between the two deepened, and they reached an understanding they would marry. On one of Hawthorne's many visits to see Elizabeth, her sister Sophia, who had been plagued by headaches, ventured downstairs, and instantly recognized in the author her soul mate. Hawthorne reciprocated her interest. Elizabeth complained that Sophia was intruding in her relationship with Nathaniel by accepting so many visits from him. Caught between the affections of these two admirers, Hawthorne, like his alter ego Wakefield, vanished for a time. He wrote to Sophia, who relayed the message to Elizabeth:

> He was not going to tell anyone where he was going to be the next three months—that he thought he should change his name so that if he died no one would be able to find his grave stone. He would not tell even his mother where he could be found—that he neither intended to write to anyone nor be written to.[14]

Could Hawthorne have taken lodgings in the next street over, bought a wig of reddish hair, selected "sundry garments, in a fashion unlike his customary brown," and become an "Outcast of the Universe," like the "crafty nincompoop" of whom he had written?

By 1839 Hawthorne was engaged to marry Sophia, and Elizabeth obliquely wrote of her loss: "Dissolution is painful when the attraction of cohesion ceases."[15] She nonetheless wangled for him the position of customs inspector at the Port of Boston, so that he would have more time to pursue his writing career.

Did Hawthorne trick Elizabeth into believing that he loved her, to further his career? He certainly vacated his life, as Wakefield had done, at a critical moment, and his self-banishment was just as complete as that of his enigmatic counterpart. We pick up the theme of Trickster in Hawthorne's life again when, on August 5, 1850, his path crossed Herman Melville's on Monument Mountain, in Massachusetts. (See "The Three Phantoms of Herman Melville's *Moby-Dick*," Chapter 31.)

No doubt exists, however, that Hawthorne's son Julian (1846–1934) was a thoroughbred trickster. Convicted of deceiving the public into buying worthless shares of the Hawthorne Silver and Iron Mines, Ltd., of which he was president, banking on the credibility of the family name, Julian was imprisoned in the Federal Penitentiary, Atlanta, Georgia, for a year and a day in 1912—one way, perhaps, of getting back at his father, in whose shadow he resentfully lived, by sullying the family name.

Outcast of the Universe

An observation in *The Scarlet Letter* appears applicable to the Hathorne-Hawthorne family psychodynamics:

> The wrong doing of one generation lives into successive ones, and, divesting itself of every temporary advantage, becomes a pure and uncontrollable mischief.[16]

The Trickster appears to surface periodically in the Hawthorne family. It can first be seen in Judge Hathorne's devilish adjudications at the witchcraft trials. We find it at a later date in Hawthorne's tangled fandango with the Peabody sisters; in his craftiness, projected into the personality of Wakefield. It resurfaces in the presence of this attribute in the character of his son Julian, whose incarceration in the United States Federal Penitentiary in Atlanta corresponds, in some way, to his father's mental dungeon under the attic eaves in Salem, forty years before.

Each male descendant of this lineage was, in one way or another, like Wakefield, an "Outcast of the Universe."

A Recurrent Nightmare

Hawthorne suffered from a recurrent nightmare periodically throughout his life and reported the "singular dream" while he was U.S. consul in Liverpool, a political appointment provided by Franklin Pierce, the fourteenth president of the United States, a Bowdoin College classmate, for whom Hawthorne had written a campaign biography.

He reported the dream in his journal, the only ongoing literary activity in which Hawthorne was engaged at the time.

> December 28th, 1854. For a long, long while, I have occasionally been visited with a singular dream; and I have an impression that I have dreamed it ever since I have been in England. It is that I am still at college—or, sometimes even at school—and there is a sense that I have been there unconsciously long, and have quite failed to make such progress in life as my contemporaries have; and I seem to meet some of them with a feeling of *shame and depression* that broods over me, when I think of it, even at this moment. This dream, recurring all through these twenty or thirty years, must be one of the effects of that heavy seclusion in which I shut myself up for twelve years, after leaving college, when everybody moved onward and left me behind.[17]

Because he was earning more money in the consulate than ever before, had achieved a modicum of literary success and was surrounded by family, Hawthorne was understandably perplexed by the timing of the nightmare's recurrence:

> How strange that it should come now, when I call myself famous and prosperous!—when I am happy, too!—still that same dream of life hopelessly a failure."[18]

Writing and Self-Dialogue

Hawthorne overlooked the importance that writing had for his mental well-being, allowing him to be in touch with his innermost feelings. From the time he had become U.S. consul, he had been unable to write, believing that the job was incompatible with artistic endeavors.

Malcolm Cowley, editor of *The Portable Hawthorne*, describes the way the author told his tales. A "loner," who once admitted he had at most a dozen intimate conversations with others in the course of his entire life, he had, however, regular conversations with himself. Cowley writes:

> Hawthorne seems to have divided himself into two personalities while dreaming out his stories; one was the storyteller and the other the audience. The storyteller uttered his stream of silent words; the audience listened and applauded by a sort of inner glow, or criticized by means of an invisible form that seemed to say, "But I don't understand." "Let me go over that again," the storyteller would answer, still soundlessly, and then would repeat his tale in clearer language, with more details, and perhaps repeat the doubtful passages again and again, till he was sure the invisible listener would understand.[19]

Hawthorne's association of the recurrent nightmare to the "heavy seclusion" of the postcollege years when he was in a "mental dungeon" is significant. During those years, he also perceived himself as "undistinguished." Only by writing could he distinguish himself. Writing literally vitalized him.

After returning from England, Hawthorne tried writing a novel whose protagonist, Septimius Felton, killed another man who was in possession of a secret formula for eternal life. In the course of writing it, the author developed a writer's block, was unable to complete the book, and once again lost touch with his feelings, particularly the shameful ones. Hawthorne felt he could "no longer plod along with the multitude. . . . Impatient as regards this earthly life, since it is coming to an end, I do not try to be contented, but weary of it while it lasts."

Unable to participate in self-dialogue as a writer, he reentered the mental dungeon of the nonparticipant observer, like Wakefield, and died psychically incarcerated.

NOTES

1. Nathaniel Hawthorne, *Tales*, J. McIntosh, ed., (New York: Norton, 1987), 75–76.

2. Ibid., 76.

3. To H. W. Longfellow, June 4, 1837, ibid., 297.

4. J. Mellow, *Nathaniel Hawthorne*, Boston: Houghton Mifflin, 1980, 11.

5. Hawthorne, 77. Emphasis added.

6. Ibid., 79. Emphasis added.

7. Ibid., 77.

8. Ibid., 76.

9. Ibid., 79. Emphasis added.

10. Ibid., 76.

11. Megan Marshall, *The Peabody Sisters: Three Women Who Ignited American Romanticism*. New York: Houghton Mifflin, 2005, 355.

12. Ibid., 254.

13. Ibid.

14. Ibid.

15. Ibid., 367.

16. Hawthorne, "Preface," *The Scarlet Letter* (1850).

17. Hawthorne, *English Notebooks*, Dec. 28, 1854. In Malcolm Cowley, ed., *The Portable Hawthorne*, New York: Viking Press, 1974, 643–44. Emphasis added.

18. Ibid., 644.

19. Ibid., 6–7.

Chapter Twenty-One

Frederick Law Olmsted's Childhood Traumas and the Birth of Psychoarchitecture

Frederick Law Olmsted (1822–1903) was a visionary landscape architect whose firm shaped many of America's open spaces. Between 1857 and 1950, the Olmsted company participated in some 5,500 projects,[1] including New York City's Central Park, the Niagara Falls reservation, Yale University, the United States Capitol grounds, Yosemite Valley, California's Stanford University campus, and Harvard-affiliated McLean Hospital, whose site Olmsted selected in 1872 and to which, twenty-five years later, he returned as a patient.

In his early years he sustained a series of traumas that impacted significantly on his life, prolonging his search for a vocational identity, leading him to explore the possibilities of psychoarchitecture, and perhaps contributing to his psychiatric hospitalization.

The major trauma was his mother's death from an overdose of laudanum following an extensive postpartum depression. Olmsted described the dreadful experience in two sentences in an undated autobiographical fragment that succinctly conveys his terror and suggests the presumptive psychiatric diagnosis of a stress disorder:

> When I was three years old I chanced to stray into a room at the crisis of a tragedy therein occurring and turned and fled from it screaming in a manner adding to the horror of the household. It was long before I could be soothed and those nearby said to one another that I would never forget what I had seen.[2]

Those nearby were correct, and other significant stressors followed. When his father remarried fourteen months later, the stepmother virtually banished young Olmsted from home. His care was delegated to a succession of teachers and rural clergymen, and during that time he endured further traumas. At seven, a teacher whose clothes caught on fire burned to death. A stepsister died from measles three years later. Between nine and fourteen, he boarded with a physically abusive pastor. When students were delinquent, "he was likely to rush among them and beat them with random fury over head and shoulders with a broomstick, firewood, ruler or what ever came to hand, shouting as he did so, 'Oh the depravity of human nature.'"[3]

Throughout these years his younger brother was allowed to remain at home.

In these stressful days of his youth, Frederick was fortunately able to roam through woods, field, and stream. He found nature, especially trees, restorative, perhaps from an association of trees with his mother:

> My mother died while I was so young that I have but a tradition of memory rather than the faintest recollection of her. While I was a small school boy if I was asked if I remembered her I could say, "Yes; I remember playing on the grass and looking up at her while she sat sewing under a tree. . . . [I]t has always been a delight to me to see a woman sitting under a tree, sewing and minding a child."[4]

Trees, even those that had been maltreated and were stunted, would always be uplifting to Olmsted's chronically stressed psyche, perhaps through his identification with them:

> Looking down upon [the sight of such trees] I say it is not beautiful. But looking up at the continuous canopy which these trunks support, swaying in the light summer breeze against the serene blue beyond—swaying not only with the utmost grace of motion but with the utmost stately majesty . . . if the result is not to be called beautiful it is only because it has more of sublimity than beauty.[5]

Trees were the natural objects most closely associated with his mother and it could be said that he landscaped nature to provide himself with the mother and home he did not have after three years of age. Indeed, in his holistic and psychologically oriented biography, Melvin Kalfus ably demonstrates how Olmsted drew upon deep, unfulfilled emotional needs in evolving his idea of urban landscape architecture, idealizing nature as a mother-image, a nurturing home environment he imagined he had lost with the death of his mother.

THE PROLONGED SEARCH FOR A VOCATIONAL IDENTITY

Olmsted sought a vocational identity from the age of eighteen, when he called a halt to his father's misguided efforts to provide him with what amounted to a wretched education. Then, drifting from job to job, he worked as a businessman, scientific farmer, merchant seaman, university student, antislavery writer, and newspaper and magazine correspondent (cofounding the *Nation*). He was, he wrote, "a loitering, self-indulgent, dilettante sort of a man."[6] It is curious how two fortuitous events, occurring seven years apart, helped him to finally crystallize a vocational identity at the age of thirty-five.

The first occurred in 1850, when, after abandoning a farm in Connecticut purchased for him by his father, the twenty-eight-year-old Olmsted joined his brother and a friend on a walking trip to Europe and the continent.

He was savoring a bun in a Liverpool bakery when the proprietor suggested a side trip to Birkenhead Public Park, designed by Joseph Paxton, the future architect of London's Crystal Palace. Paxton had totally transformed 120 acres of flat clay farmland by digging a lake and using the excavated earth to create rolling hills, meadows, shady glens, overgrown hillocks, and footpaths that meandered through clumps of leafy trees.

This pluperfect scene captured Olmsted's imagination: "We stood dumbstricken by its loveliness," he wrote.[7] And in an essay for the *Horticulturist* he detailed the underground drainage system that fed water to the lake, and noted such features as the artful composition of the winding paths.

Olmsted was interested in landscaping in order to improve the lot of all classes of people living in cities. Birkenhead sought to do just this, and he bemoaned the absence of comparable parks in the United States. In his first published psychoarchitectural statement, he described the impact of landscape architecture on the human psyche.[8]

Seven years later, at a resort in New Haven, Connecticut, Olmsted met a commissioner who was planning Central Park. He learned that the position of project superintendent, dealing with design and construction, was open. Olmsted, it appears in retrospect, was waiting for the opportunity to put Birkenhead's principles into the plan. He applied and was chosen for the post, partly based on his essay in the *Horticulturist* and partly on his literary connections.

Successful in this first major public work, Olmsted had finally found his calling: landscape psychoarchitecture. "If a fairy had shaped it for me," he wrote, "it could not have fitted me better. It was normal, ordinary, and naturally outgrowing from my previous life history."[9]

The psychologist Erik Erikson's concept of the "psychosocial moratorium" comes to mind when one considers Olmsted's circuitous path to a career identity. Erickson's term designates the frame of time, sometimes prolonged in gifted people, that is required to organize their own particular niche in society.

By introducing nature into the urban scene, Olmsted offered saunterers relief from the psychopathologic influences of city life, "the symptoms of which," he wrote, "are nervous tension, over-anxiety, hasteful disposition, impatience, [and] irritability."[10] Olmsted knew from his own experience that such symptoms could be reversed through exposure to pleasing rural arboreal scenery: "It is thus, in medical phrase, a prophylactic and therapeutic agent of value."[11]

At the end of a distinguished career, Olmsted reflected on the possible unconscious determinants of his psychoarchitectural landscapes. If he was aware of them, he saw no reason to publicize his insights:

> The sum is that I put into [my projects] a degree of devotion that no greed and no selfish ambition would have induced. Why—how I came to—does not concern the public. It is not necessary that you [his biographer] should fully understand it. The fact is that there was an artistic devotion in the early . . . work such that a political work or whorl of war, seldom engages, and something of this fact it may well be the public should recognize.[12]

Olmsted's medical record is sealed, but whatever his subsequent diagnosis, it is superimposed on the early post-traumatic stress disorder.

If the art of living is the ability to use life's inevitable adversities constructively, it could be said that many of us are the beneficiaries of Olmsted's landscape psychoarchitectural artistry.

NOTES

1. Frederick Law Olmsted, *The Masterlist of Design Projects of the Olmsted Firm, 1857–1950*. Boston: Mass. Association of Parks, 1987.

2. Olmsted, *Autobiographical Fragment*. In Witold Rybczynski, *A Clearing in the Distance: Frederick Law Olmsted and America in the Nineteenth Century* (New York, Scribner's, 1999), 23–24.

3. Cf. F. L. Olmsted, Jr., and T. Kimball, eds., *Frederick Law Olmsted, Landscape Architect, 1833–1903* (New York: Putnam's, 1922), 57.

4. Melvin Kalfus, *Frederick Law Olmsted: The Passion of a Public Artist*, New York, New York University Press, 1990, 132.

5. Ibid., 135.

6. Ibid., 149.

7. Ibid., 159.

8. F. L. Olmsted, "The People's Park at Birkenhead, near Liverpool," *The Horticulturist*, May 1851, 225–26.

9. F. L. Olmsted to C. Vaux, Nov. 26, 1893, qtd. Kalfus, 185.

10. F. L. Olmsted, "Notes on the plan of Franklin Park and Related Matters" (1886), *Papers of Frederick Law Olmsted, Supplementary Series I: Writings on Public Parks, Parkways, and Park Systems* (Baltimore: Johns Hopkins University Press, 1997), 197.

11. F. L. Olmsted, *Mount Royal, Montreal* (New York: Putnam's, 1881), 22.

12. Qtd. in Laura Wood Roper, *FLO: A biography of Frederick Law Olmsted*, Baltimore: Johns Hopkins University Press, 1973.

Chapter Twenty-Two

Leo Tolstoy's "God Sees the Truth, but Waits": Through Suffering Comes Redemption

Leo Tolstoy (1828–1910) regarded "God Sees the Truth, But Waits," in which he used the artistic mastery acquired in writing *War and Peace*, as one of his finest stories. It is told with such great simplicity and is so tightly constructed that its theme—through suffering comes redemption—may be clearly understood by the young and old in all nations, from all social classes.

Ivan Aksenov, the good-looking, fun-loving hero, is a successful merchant, with two shops and a house of his own. He is married, full of fun, and very fond of singing. This first part of his life comes to an abrupt end when he is unjustly accused of murdering a man.

Aksenov is flogged for this crime and sentenced to hard labor in a Siberian prison. Instead of becoming bitter and hardened, however, he begins a spiritual journey. After twenty-six years (the "wait" to which the title refers) the true murderer, Makar Semyonych, arrives at the same prison. Both men are transformed by their encounter.

A generation later, in another part of the world, Aksenov's nonfictional counterpart, Alger Hiss, the tall, handsome, brilliant president of the Carnegie Endowment for International Peace, is accused of a crime (spying for the Soviet Union) of which many consider him innocent.

The accuser, Whittaker Chambers, a fat man with bad teeth in a rumpled suit, does not resemble Makar Semyonych physically nor does he undergo the latter's spiritual transformation, but there are certain mental similarities. Hiss and Chambers are discussed in the chapter following this one.

IVAN AKSENOV: A "FAIR-HAIRED, CURLY-HEADED FELLOW, FULL OF FUN"

Ivan Aksenov, at the beginning of the tale, is young, happy and successful. He lives in the town of Vladimir, outside of Moscow, and one day decides to go to a fair in another town to sell his wares despite his wife's admonitions. She dreamed that when he returned, his hair had become completely gray.

Halfway to the fair, he meets a merchant friend with whom he stays overnight in adjoining rooms at an inn. During the night a thief enters, robs and murders Aksenov's companion, hides the knife in Aksenov's luggage, and flees.

The next day Aksenov, unaware of the slaying, gets an early start and stops to feed himself and his horse after about twenty miles. Suddenly, the district police inspector arrives in a troika, informs him that the other merchant was murdered, and, searching Ivan's trunk, finds a bloodstained knife. Ivan is jailed and when his wife visits, she questions her husband's innocence.

Burying his face in his hands and sobbing, Ivan comes to a realization: "It seems that only God can know the truth; it is to Him alone we must appeal, and from Him alone expect mercy."[1] He is flogged mercilessly and sent to Siberia, and soon he abandons hope that the injustice will ever be rectified.

His mirth ceases in Siberia. He prays, reads the Gospel, and sings in the choir (his voice is still good); his hair turns white (as his wife dreamt); and he becomes known as a fair-minded man. He learns to make boots and with the money earned buys *The Lives of the Saints,* which he reads whenever there is sufficient light.

ENTER THE KILLER: "A TALL, STRONG MAN WITH A GREY BEARD"

One day a new group of prisoners arrives and among them is a man from Vladimir, Makar Semyonych, "a tall, strong man of sixty, with a closely-cropped grey beard." Aksenov asks him if he has heard about a murdered merchant from those parts, and the newcomer replies:

> How could I help hearing? The world's full of rumours. But it's a long time ago, and I've forgotten what I heard. . . . It must have been him in whose bag the knife was found! If some one else hid the knife there, "He's not a thief till he's caught," as the saying is. How could any one put a knife into your bag while it was under your head? It would surely have woke you up.[2]

Aware that the new convict knows what only the murderer could know, Ivan is almost certain that Makar killed the merchant. He has flashbacks of his wife and children before the shocking events, the flogging, and of his twenty-six years as a prisoner. He feels depressed and vindictive, wanting to end his life or get revenge, and cannot sleep.

Ivan avoids contact with Makar but two weeks later notices someone digging a tunnel under the wall to escape. It is Makar, who threatens to kill him if he "squeals," but offers to take him along if he keeps his mouth shut. Ivan replies: "I have no wish to escape, and you have no need to kill me; you killed me long ago! As to telling of you—I may do so or not, as God shall direct."[3]

GOD'S WILL AND GOD'S TRUTH, ALL IN GOD'S TIME

When the authorities discover the tunnel, they ask Ivan, aware that he is a truthful man, if he knows who dug it. He ponders a long time. If he reveals the name of the person, that man would be flogged and how would that improve his own life? Glancing at Makar, he tells the Governor: "I cannot say, your honour. It is not God's will that I should tell!"[4]

That night Makar, moved by Ivan's protection of him, approaches his bed and begs forgiveness: "It was I who killed the merchant and hid the knife among your things. I meant to kill you too, but I heard a noise outside, so I hid the knife in your bag and escaped out of the window." Makar wants to confess to the murder so that Ivan can be freed and go home, but Ivan replies, "Where could I go to now? My wife is dead, and my children have forgotten me. I have nowhere to go."[5]

When Makar pleads for forgiveness and bursts out sobbing, Ivan also begins to weep. "God will forgive you!" said he. "Maybe I am a hundred times worse than you."[6] Then his heart becomes lighter. Makar confesses to the authorities that he committed the murder, but when official permission comes for Ivan's release, he is dead.

The story may be divided into two halves. In the first half, Aksenov is happily married, full of fun, enjoys singing, has two shops and a house and is glad to be alive. When his wife disbelieves his innocence, he is shocked and despairs of finding justice on earth.

In the second half, his appearance is totally different. He has a long, thin, gray beard; his mirth is gone; he walks slowly with a stoop, rarely talks, and never laughs. He has lost contact with family and has no worldly possessions.

Aksenov has begun a twenty-six-year spiritual journey following a shocking injustice. Starting from a state of mirthfulness, in the subsequent two and a half decades, he experiences despair, resignation, and bitterness, and finally finds acceptance and through it contentment and liberation.

If God has seen the truth, one may ask, why does He wait? Perhaps Tolstoy believed that Aksenov's spiritual awakening was gradual and would only be complete when it impacted on the scapegrace Makar, who, profoundly touched by his protector's compassion, also has a spiritual awakening.

This is consistent with Tolstoy's statement in his essay *What Is Art?*: "The business of art consists precisely in making comprehensible and accessible that which might be incomprehensible and inaccessible in the form of reasoned explanation."[7]

NOTES

1. Leo Tolstoy, "God Sees the Truth, but Waits." (Reprinted from Thomas Seltzer, ed., *Best Russian Short Stories*, New York: Boni & Liveright, 1917.) Short Story Archive, http://www.shortstoryarchive.com/t/god_sees_the_truth_but_waits.html — Accessed Mar. 27, 2009.

2. Ibid.

3. Ibid.

4. Ibid.

5. Ibid.

6. Ibid.

7. Tolstoy, *What is Art?* R. Pevear and L. Volokhonsky, tr. (New York: Penguin Books, 1995), 81.

Chapter Twenty-Three

Alger Hiss and Whittaker Chambers:
A Real-life Ivan and Makar

ALGER HISS'S BRILLIANT PAST
AND SEEMINGLY AUSPICIOUS FUTURE

Alger Hiss (1904–1996) as a young man was tall, slim, dapper, and brilliant. At Johns Hopkins University, where he belonged to Phi Beta Kappa, he was voted the "most popular student" by his 1926 graduating class. He attended Harvard Law School, clerked for Supreme Court Justice Oliver Wendell Holmes, married, and had children.

He entered government service in 1933, working for the Departments of Agriculture and Justice. In 1936 he joined the State Department and rose so rapidly that by 1945 he was an advisor to President Roosevelt at Yalta, then secretary general of the United Nations Charter Conference in San Francisco. The following year he became president of the Carnegie Foundation for International Peace.

As in the life of Tolstoy's fictional Aksenov, all this abruptly ended halfway through his life when, in 1948, Whittaker Chambers, senior editor of *Time* magazine and a former Communist Party courier, appeared before the House of Representatives Un-American Activities Committee claiming that ten years before, Hiss passed on to him State Department secrets, which Chambers, in turn, passed on to the Soviet Union.

Hiss denied the accusation. Nonetheless, there was a federal grand jury investigation, in which a young congressman named Richard Nixon vigorously pursued him, and he was charged with perjury. A first trial in 1949 ended with a hung jury, but the following year, a second jury found Hiss guilty and he was sentenced to five years in a federal penitentiary. Many believe that the Federal Bureau of Investigation tampered with the evidence to secure a conviction.

Chambers went on to write his memoirs; Nixon, an obscure congressman from California, was catapulted to fame and the White House after the Hiss inquisition; the trials set the stage for Senator Joseph McCarthy's Communist witch hunts and ushered in an era of political and intellectual conservatism that led to Ronald Reagan's presidency; and Hiss served time in Lewisburg.

When released from prison, the term shortened for good conduct, Hiss spent the rest of his life trying to clear his name. With the collapse of communism in Russia, he attempted to obtain information from Soviet intelligence files. Hiss wrote to Dimitry Volkogonov, the overseer of the Soviet intelligence archives, requesting the release of any files about him. In 1992, Volkogonov published a report that he found no evidence Hiss had ever been an agent for the KGB, GRU, or any other intelligence agency of the Soviet Union.

Freedom from the Mental Jail

Both Aksenov and Hiss began a mental and spiritual journey in prison. Aksenov learned to make boots, earned a little money, and with it bought his only reading matter. On Sundays he read the Gospel in the prison chapel and sang hymns in the choir.

Hiss also used the time to learn and grow. In the realm of ethics, for example, he wrote:

> There was the occasion for a reconsideration of first principles, of values, of objectives, and I welcomed the occasion. I had lived so actively that the reflective side of my nature had only occasional chances to assess basic considerations and motivations."[1]

He derived enormous satisfaction by helping others and, for example, described the way he taught one inmate (B.R. for "beginning reader") to read and write:

> The B.R.'s progress in his studies—he can now spell and write over 350 words—[is remarkable]. . . . His wife will be very pleased and proud—this will be the first time she has ever seen his handwriting.[2]

When B.R. was transferred to another prison unit, Hiss recognized the psychological value of his endeavors: "It is good for him to realize that he no longer needs help, but on the contrary can give it." Per the old adage, Hiss had taught B.R. to fish, not just given him a meal.

During the incarceration, Hiss's mental and spiritual growth was incontestable. His son, Tony, writes:

> Lewisburg did not perfect Alger, but it is where his best self grew; he entered prison as an expert in foreign policy and international organization, and left possessing a deep-intuitive understanding of many oddly assorted areas.[3]

A stepson, Tim Hobson, concurred:

> I think the playful side of Alger got buried alive sometime during his childhood. . . . Alger died a happier man with Lewisburg behind him—he got closer to other people, he got closer to his soul. Jail is a funny place to come up for air in your life, but jail is where Alger became a human being.[4]

Even before his incarceration, Hiss shared his time, energy, and intelligence with others. As law clerk to Justice Holmes, he read aloud to his beloved, aging mentor—an hour a day if the court was in session, three hours daily if not. He was the first law clerk to accompany Holmes to his Beverly Farms, Massachusetts, home during the Court's summer recess, and he continued to read to Holmes long after the law clerkship passed on to others.

Holmes, in many ways, was the father lost to him in childhood. "The Justice in Boston," Hiss noted in a letter to his wife, "told me he told F.F. [Felix Frankfurter, who arranged the law clerkship] [that it was as if] he'd been my father whom I not only loved, but whose society I enjoy."[5]

Hiss noted Holmes's "immediate intensity and fullness of focus in all personal relations—no divided or wandering mind for him. That quality, so notable in his talk, informs the letters with his warm and vital personality—hard of head and sensitive of spirit."

What Hiss learned from Holmes, he later put into effect in prison, and after his release he emulated his mentor. A friend in the post-prison years observed:

> Pain and disappointment never seemed to dominate his life. Rather, what I saw was excitement about a new book, passion about the events of the day, and pleasure—easily and warmly expressed—in friendship. The fineness of his daily contacts is what conveyed his breadth, depth, and reach.[6]

A Crippling Detachment

The key to Hiss's problems, in the opinion of his son Tony, was that "he was a person who suffered from an unwariness and a detachment that would cripple his attempts to defend himself against invented charges."[7]

This problem may have been a manifestation of a psychiatric syndrome, post-traumatic stress disorder (PTSD), discussed earlier in this book in connection with Tolstoy's Aksenov, the Unabomber, Glenn Gould, and Joyce's Gabriel Conroy. PTSD is a delayed response to an overwhelming stress in a person's life. One of its symptoms, "psychic numbing," also called "emotional anesthesia," could have produced the crippling effect his son noted.

When Alger was two and a half years old, his father committed suicide by cutting his throat with a razor. What made matters worse was that the cause of death was concealed from Hiss and his brother, who only learned of it by overhearing a neighbor's conversation.

If truth is withheld from a person by those whom he trusts, the issue of who can be trusted with what, and to what extent, arises. This problem is intertwined with another described by Hiss's son. Alger Hiss "continued to navigate through life with one sense missing. He couldn't, or couldn't let himself, sense when someone, either inadvertently or deliberately, might hurt him."[8]

Hiss experienced other traumas as well: a brother, Bosley, died in his early twenties; and a sister, Mary, committed suicide a few years later. These stressors added to the trauma of the father's suicide and its cover-up. It is reasonable to hypothesize that Hiss suffered from severe, chronic PTSD.

Throughout his prison term, Hiss used the time, undistracted by national and international affairs, to focus on intimacy in human relationships. With his "alpha-plus intellect" and the single-minded attention to detail he had learned from his "second father," Oliver Wendell Holmes, he sought ways to thaw out from the psychic numbing, the detachment that characterized his pre-prison responses. He wrote his wife:

> While I "want out" without the minutest reservation, I find that here as elsewhere there is large opportunity for learning and growing. I am experiencing prison life with full health and vigor, physically and mentally.[9]

Cultivating relationships in jail with people whom he hadn't met at Harvard, the State Department, or the Carnegie Foundation, Hiss was able to write his son:

> Happiness is a natural result of a full and healthy growing. In that respect men and women and children are like flowers; when they are healthy they grow continually—and they blossom. The blossom is our happiness.[10]

By helping others in the penitentiary, such as the beginning reader, Hiss blossomed. When Aksenov refused to "squeal" on the man responsible for over two and a half decades of imprisonment, Makar Semyonych confessed to the crime. Both Hiss and Aksenov learned equanimity during their incarcerations, developed spiritual power, and never became vindictive.

Aksenov and Hiss led the first half of their lives without being conscious of their spiritual nature. The way in which they responded to the dreadful traumas in their lives enabled their spirituality to grow.

Although Tolstoy believed that "through suffering comes redemption," one person was apparently untouched by the tumultuous events in the same way as the other three—Whittaker Chambers. Dr. Carl Binger, a psychiatrist who testified in the perjury trials, considered that Chambers had "a psychopathic personality"[11] and was given to mental delusions, like a Marxist Walter Mitty, prone to fabricating fantastic tales about himself and others.

Chambers wrote of himself: "I am an outcast. My family is outcast. We have no friends, no social ties, no church, and no organization that we claim and that claims us, no community." He had written of Hiss's "great gentleness and sweetness of character" and of his "unnumbered little acts of kindness and affection."[12]

An observation made by Tony Hiss about Chambers is pertinent:

> I've thought that perhaps Chambers felt drawn to my father not because he wanted to be with him but because he wished he could somehow be him, and possess his serenity.[13]

Tom Ripley's responses to Dickie Greenleaf in *The Talented Mr. Ripley* come to mind. Working in a men's rest room; living in a rundown basement apartment; having no girlfriend, art, or money in his life; and then encountering Dickie Greenleaf, who he felt had everything he lacked—it all creates overwhelming envy. Tom murders Dickie and assumes his identity, luxuriating in the new life.

While Chambers did not murder Hiss, toppling him from the presidency of the Carnegie Endowment for International Peace to incarceration in a federal penitentiary led to the death of Hiss's former self. Fortunately, the latter discovered, like Aksenov and Dr. Martin Luther King, Jr. (to whom we turn in chapter 25), that "unmerited suffering is redemptive."[14] Unfortunately, this spiritual lesson was not learned by Whittaker Chambers or, as you may recall, by Nathaniel Hawthorne's antihero, Wakefield.

The distinction may be made between prison, which Ivan Aksenov and Makar Semyonych, Dr. King, Hiss and Gandhi all inhabited, and the mental jail, in which Chambers, Wakefield, Ripley, the Unabomber, and Conrad's Lord Jim dwelled. Here is a poem I wrote, which describes their differences:

Prison and the Mental Jail

Prison is an island of iron bars, barbed wire and armed guards
Surrounded by an ocean of time.

The mental jail, without physical constraints,
Is far more confining.
Built of bricks of guilt and shame, anxiety and fear,
Rage, anger and feelings of despair,
Its ceiling is too low to stand tall and proud,
Its walls too narrow to breathe easily,
Its cells too short to stretch out and relax.
Deconstruction is possible:
Firmly grasp the bricks
And stack them as steps to climb.
At the top, the mental jail is seen as
A palace of wisdom surrounded by a garden.
Cultivate what grows best in your own soil.[15]

One of Thoreau's observations comes to mind: "If we will be quiet and ready enough, we shall find compensation in every disappointment."[16]

NOTES

1. Tony Hiss, *The View from Alger's Window: a Son's Memoir* (New York: Knopf, 1999), 144.

2. Ibid., 170–71.

3. Ibid., 225–26.

4. Ibid., 221–22.

5. Ibid., 136–37

6. Ibid., 240.

7. Ibid., 82.

8. Ibid., 226–27.

9. Ibid., 126.

10. Ibid., 230.

11. John Earl Haynes and Harvey Klehr. *Early Cold War Spies: The Espionage Trials that Shaped American Politics* (Cambridge: Cambridge University Press, 2006), 127.

12. Whittaker Chambers, *Witness* (New York: Random House, 1952), 148, 70.

13. Hiss, 202.

14. King's words in his Birmingham, Alabama, eulogy (1961). Cf. David R. Goldfield, *Black, White, and Southern: Race Relations and Southern Culture, 1940 to the Present* (LSU Press, 1991). 144.

15. Published in *Psychiatric Times* (2002).

16. Thoreau, *Journal*, ed. cit., 1:60.

Chapter Twenty-Four

Henry David Thoreau's "Wilderness Therapy": Sensory Awareness in Nature

"It is the marriage of soul with Nature that makes the intellect fruitful, that gives birth to imagination."

—Thoreau, Journal, August 21, 1851

Henry David Thoreau, who (as we saw earlier in this volume) suffered from severe post-traumatic stress disorder (PTSD), found that "the marriage of soul with nature" was restorative. He detailed his practice, which could be called "wilderness therapy," in journal entries on two anniversaries of his brother's shocking death. Our overmedicated society may take interest in the drug-free solution he devised to deal with PTSD.

REAL TETANUS AND FACSIMILE TETANUS

On New Year's Day, 1842, Henry Thoreau's beloved older brother, John Thoreau, Jr., sliced off the tip of his ring finger while stropping his razor. He replaced the severed piece, staunched the flow of blood with a cloth, and bandaged the wound.

A few days later he began experiencing pain. On January 8, he went to the doctor but his pain was so intense that it was difficult for him to make his way home. By morning, trismus—tetanic spasms of the muscles of mastication causing rigid jaw closure ("lockjaw")—set in.

It is difficult to depict the ghastly, grotesque nature of death from tetanus: suffocation due to paralysis of the respiratory muscles, jaws locked, and lips drawn back in a "sardonic grin" (*risus sardonicus*) from facial-musculature spasm. When the dreadful nature of the terminal state is conveyed, the severity of Henry's subsequent stress disorder may be fully grasped.

John was virtually the only person in Henry's life whom he loved, admired, and trusted. Henry, a devoted and attentive caretaker throughout his illness, held John in his arms as he died.

On January 22, eleven days later, Henry also developed symptoms of lockjaw, and doctors were afraid he would also die, although they found no skin breaks where the microorganism *Clostridium tetanii* could lodge, form a spore, and release its deadly neurotoxin. On the twenty-fourth, he gradually recovered from facsimile lockjaw, a manifestation of acute stress disorder. But symptoms of chronic post-traumatic stress disorder (PTSD) developed.

PTSD, a cluster of symptoms that may follow such a life-threatening trauma, includes the "anniversary phenomenon," a (usually annual) reactivation of some of the symptoms that occurred at the time of the initial trauma.

Thoreau experienced the depression, anxiety, and irritability of the "anniversary phenomena" at the time of his brother's death and on anniversaries of it throughout his life. He devised what I call "wilderness therapy" to deal with the symptoms. Basically, it involved sensory awareness—special attention, in the present moment, to what one can see, hear, touch, taste, and smell in nature. It is difficult to ruminate about a grotesque death when intently focused on what is sensible in the "here and now." The phenomenon is described by Thoreau on two of John's death anniversaries.

December 31, 1853: Sensory Awareness and an Out-of-Body Experience

The day before the New Year around the eleventh anniversary of John's fatal wound, four inches of snow had fallen around Walden Pond by the time Thoreau began his walk. The activity of the brain during this sequence of sensory activities helps explain why such practices are therapeutic.

The first of the five senses that catches Thoreau's attention on his pond-side walk is the *visual*:

> It is a remarkable sight, this snow-clad landscape, with the fences and bushes half buried and the warm sun on it. The snow lies not quite level in the fields, but in low waves with an abrupt edge on the north or wind side, as it lodges on ice.[1]

The penetrating silence following a snowfall is interrupted by a shrill *auditory* stimulus:

> The town and country are now so still, there being no rattle of wagons nor even jingle of sleigh-bells, every tread being as with woolen feet, I hear very

distinctly from the railroad causeway the whistle of the locomotive on the Lowell road.[2]

He has several associations to the whistle. A cock crowing on this type of a day, he writes, is heard from afar for the same reason. Then, he notes, a few sounds never fail to move him: "The notes of the wood thrush and the sound of a vibrating chord, these affect me as many sounds once did often, and as almost all should."

The strains of the wood thrush and the Aeolian (wind-activated) harp, he finds, "are the truest and loftiest preachers. . . . I know of no missionaries to us heathen comparable to them."

This elicits the *tactile* association: "They, as it were, lift us up in spite of ourselves. They intoxicate, they charm us. . . . I would be drunk, drunk, drunk, dead drunk to this world with it forever."

Next, Thoreau has an association to *taste*: "Where was that strain mixed into which this world was dropped but as a lump of sugar to sweeten the draught?"

Returning to sound, Thoreau associates it to the sensation of taste:

> He that hath ears, let him hear. The contact of sound with a human ear whose hearing is pure and unimpaired is coincident with an ecstasy. Sugar is not so sweet to the palate, as sound to the healthy ear.[3]

He explores the relation of sound, first to courage: "The hearing of it [sound] makes men brave." Then, responding to such sounds, Thoreau has an out-of-body experience: "It, as it were, takes me out of my body and gives me the freedom of all bodies and all nature."[4]

The last of the five senses, *olfaction*, appears in the final word of the passage, in which Thoreau describes the culmination of his wilderness therapy: "I leave my body in a trance and accompany the zephyr and the fragrance."[5]

The next day, Thoreau quotes from an account of the death of a young Frenchwoman who had devoted her entire life to the "savages" of Canada: "Finally this beautiful soul detached itself from its body. . ."[6] Unconsciously, Thoreau may not only have been writing about himself, but about his brother, and also about the possibility of his spirit joining his brother's: "It . . . takes me out of my body and gives me the freedom of all bodies. . ."[7]

Mind and Brain at Walden Pond

It is possible to track the activities of the brain during this "anniversary" walk. Since Thoreau's journal entry begins, "It is a remarkable sight, this snow-clad landscape,"[8] the brain region processing incoming visual stimuli, the principal visual cortex of the occipital lobe, is the first to receive an incoming electrical impulse.

Next, the part of the brain that processes sound, the primary auditory cortex of the temporal lobe, is activated when a locomotive whistle penetrates the silence of the countryside. Thoreau's reflections on it—"I frequently mistake at first a very distant whistle for the higher tones of the telegraph harp"[9] (the vibrating telegraph wires)—result from a stimulation of the associative auditory cortex.

The impulse then activates the parietal lobe's primary sensory cortex, and the association areas of the parietal lobe involved in proprioception, when Thoreau states the sounds "lift him up." Proprioception, the awareness of the body's orientation in space, results from the integration of several sensory systems, including input from skin, muscles, and tendons; visual and motor input from the brain; and sensory data from the inner ear.

Certain meditative states, such as the one Thoreau entered on his winter walk, dissociate the conscious brain from proprioceptive input, and may lead to disembodied feelings of floating or rising. Out-of-body experiences such as the one reported may result from a temporary redistribution of electrical activity.

The feelings of well-being relate from the bypass of overused brain regions (the prefrontal region where thinking occurs) to sensory association areas.

January 7, 1857: An Imaginary Companion, a Recurrent Nightmare, and Insanity

It is the fifth day of bitter cold on the sixth anniversary of John's death, and Thoreau, as usual on such occasions, is out in Walden woods. He reports: "There is nothing so sanative, so poetic, as a walk in the woods and fields. . . . Nothing so inspires me and excites sure serene and profitable thought. The objects are elevated. . . . I come to myself, I once more feel myself grandly related."[10] What went on in Thoreau's psyche to lead to such feelings of oneness?

"I get away a mile or two from the town into the stillness and solitude of nature,"[11] Thoreau writes, so the primary auditory cortex is the first region of the brain that is stimulated.

Then he enters a glade in the woods, where a few weeds and dry leaves lift themselves above the surface of the snow, and it is as if he has come to an open window:

> I see out and around my self. Our *skylights* are thus far away from the ordinary resorts of men. I am not satisfied with ordinary windows. I must have a true *skylight*. My true sky light is on the outside of the village.[12]

In the Walden woods, which Thoreau frequented with his deceased brother, he experiences a presence: "It is as if I always met in those places some grand serene, immortal, infinitely encouraging, though invisible, companion, and walked with him."[13]

Encountering this presence is therapeutic for the post-traumatic stress disorder, producing this reunion fantasy:

> There at last my nerves are steadied. . . *There*, in that Well Meadow Field, perhaps, I feel in my element again, as when a fish is put back into the water. I wash off all my chagrins.[14]

Thoreau's associations to this simile lead him to a horrible recurrent nightmare from his earliest years:

> I can remember that when I was very young I used to have a dream night after night, over and over again, which might have been named Rough and Smooth. All existence, all satisfaction and dissatisfaction, all event was symbolized in this way.[15]

He describes the nightmares in tactile terms:

> Now I seemed to be lying and tossing, perchance, on a horrible, a fatal rough surface, which must soon, indeed, put an end to my existence . . . and then again, suddenly, I was lying on a delicious smooth surface, as of a summer sea, as of gossamer or down or softest plush. . ."[16]

Then, based on the two tactile modes of his dream, Thoreau makes a startling revelation: "My waking experience *always* has been and is such an alternate Rough and Smooth. In other words it is Insanity and Sanity."[17] Through wilderness therapy, emptying mind through hearing, listening, seeing, and touching what was around and about him, he was able to recall an early childhood dream. Based on it, he self-diagnosed what is now called bipolar disorder.

Wilderness therapy was restorative to Thoreau. A week after envisioning the imaginary companion, he is back in nature and following the sight of a song sparrow taking refuge from the snow. He makes this observation:

> What is there in music that it should so stir our deeps? We are all ordinarily in a state of desperation; such is our life; ofttimes it drives us to suicide. To how many, perhaps to most, life is barely tolerable, and if it were not for the fear of death or of dying, what a multitude would immediately commit suicide! But let us hear a strain of music, we are at once advertised of a life which no man had told us of, which no preacher preaches.[18]

He tries to describe what a strain of music has "advertised" to him—a loosening of the boundaries of self:

> The field of my life becomes a boundless plain, glorious to tread, with no death nor disappointment at the end of it. All meanness and trivialness disappear. I become adequate to any deed. No particulars survive this expansion; persons do not survive it. In the light of this strain there is no thou nor I.[19]

SENSORY AWARENESS, NEUROPSYCHIATRY AND WILDERNESS THERAPY

Sensory awareness played an important role in the creative endeavors of Thoreau. We may hypothesize here that, just as a pebble, dropped in the center of a pond, sends ripples to the distant shores, so greater areas of the genius's brain are activated (the "brain set on fire") than in the average person, which facilitates the multidimensional perspective necessary to apprehend truth.

Thoreau's wilderness therapy calls to mind words of Aldous Huxley:

> To be shaken out of the ruts of ordinary perception, to be shown for a few timeless hours the outer and the inner world, not as they appear to an animal obsessed with survival or to a human being obsessed with words and notions, but as they are apprehended, directly and unconditionally, by Mind at Large—this is an experience of inestimable value to everyone and especially to the intellectual.[20]

Huxley considered the human mind a vast repository of universal information and believed that a filtering device, a type of valve, prevented it from overwhelming the organism. It could be said that Thoreau's experiences in nature enabled him to open the "valve" allowing an expanded view of reality: "The field of my life becomes a boundless plain, glorious to tread, with no death nor disappointment at the end of it. All meanness and trivialness disappear. I become adequate to any deed."[21]

NOTES

1. Thoreau, *Journal*, 6:38–39. (December 31, 1853.)
2. Ibid., 39.
3. All ibid.
4. Ibid., 40.
5. Ibid.

6. Ibid., 42. Thoreau in this passage refers to an account by Paul Lejeune, 17th-century missionary leader in Québec.

7. Ibid.

8. Ibid., 38.

9. Ibid., 39.

10. Ibid., 9:208. (Jan. 7, 1857.)

11. Ibid., 209.

12. Ibid.

13. Ibid.

14. Ibid., 209–10.

15. Ibid., 210.

16. Ibid., 210–11.

17. Ibid., 211.

18. Ibid., 222.

19. Ibid.

20. Aldous Huxley, *The Doors of Perception* and *Heaven and Hell*, HarperCollins, 2004, 73.

21. Thoreau, 222.

Chapter Twenty-Five

The Great Deeds of Henry David Thoreau, Mohandas Gandhi, and Martin Luther King, Jr.: Crisis, Preparation, and a Deliberative Moment

Among the moral achievements of the past 150 years, three of the most outstanding occurred in unpretentious settings, following a stressful crisis, to men whose minds were prepared—Henry David Thoreau, Mohandas Gandhi, and Martin Luther King, Jr. If humankind is to survive our current life-threatening predicaments (terrorism, nuclear proliferation, global warming, etc.), it makes sense to study and apply the techniques of these great problem-solvers. They were guided by the following basic precepts:

1. Crisis = Risk + Opportunity

    "Risk + opportunity" represents the combination of characters found in the Chinese ideogram meaning "crisis." A crisis always presents risks, but invariably an opportunity coexists. In the midst of the stress of crisis it is difficult to keep this in mind, and opportunities may go unrecognized. None of these three men retreated in the face of the great crisis of his life, and each was able to use it in a productive fashion that was transformative.

2. "In the field of observation, chance favors the prepared mind."—Louis Pasteur

    These men spent considerable time mentally, prior to their crisis, in preparation. The solutions that they found were not the result of "good luck."

3. "Live deliberately."—Henry David Thoreau

    Libra, the Latin root of *deliberate*, means "scale" or "balance," and Thoreau admonished us to weigh things, balance the pros and cons, before acting. In this way, we become more aware of the risks and benefits, the opportunities as well as the risks, and so may make informed decisions.

Thoreau used these words to explain his rationale for relocating to Walden Pond: "I went to the woods because I wished to live deliberately. . ."[1]

When the above three principles are coordinated, ideas are born, wherever one happens to be, as Camus observed when he wrote: "Great works are often born on a street corner or in a restaurant's revolving door."[2] This is demonstrated in the three great deeds of Thoreau, Gandhi, and King. Thoreau's pivotal moment took place on a Concord, Massachusetts, street in 1847; Gandhi's in a worker's meeting hall in Ahmadabad, India, in 1916; and King's in a kitchen, over a cup of coffee, in Montgomery, Alabama, in 1956.

Each had been grappling with an impending crisis, generating overwhelming stress in their psyches. Disregarding personal risk, they used their stress to enter a meditative or "deliberative" state in which they formed solutions to their problems.

In *The Art of Thought* (1926), the social philosopher Graham Wallas described the process of creative thinking, delineating five stages:

1. *Preparation:* Preparatory work on a problem focuses the individual's mind on the problem and explores the problem's dimensions.
2. *Incubation:* The problem is internalized into the unconscious mind and nothing appears externally to be happening.
3. *Intimation:* The creative person gets a "feeling" that a solution is on its way.
4. *Illumination or insight:* The creative idea bursts forth from its preconscious processing into conscious awareness.
5. *Verification:* The idea is consciously verified, elaborated, and then applied.

The brain mechanisms involved in the deliberative and creative thinking of these three great men are explored in the rest of this chapter.

THOREAU'S CRISIS: "WHAT MAY A MAN DO AND NOT BE ASHAMED OF IT?"

Mortifying shame was a central issue in Thoreau's life, and he consciously struggled to overcome it. Soon after graduating from college he wrote:

What may a man do and not be ashamed of it? . . . Such is man,—toiling, heaving, struggling ant-like to shoulder some stray unappropriated crumb and deposit it in his granary; . . . can he not wriggling, screwing, self-exhorting, self-constraining, wriggle or screw out something that shall live,—respected, intact, intangible, not to be sneezed at?[3]

Several problems led him to write that "a sense of unworthiness possesses me, not without reason."[4] Homoeroticism, no more socially acceptable then than it is today, surely contributed to the problem. After the twenty-year-old Thoreau wrote a homoerotic poem, "Sympathy," apparently about an eleven-year-old male student, Thoreau's mentor, Ralph Waldo Emerson, tried to cover up the subject of the poem, insisting it was about the youth's sister, although the pronouns did not correspond.[5]

Another contribution to the "sense of unworthiness" was a fire Thoreau inadvertently set, which burned down some three hundred acres of choice Concord woodlands. "For years," writes Thoreau biographer Walter Harding, "Thoreau had to endure the whisper of 'woods-burner' behind his back."[6]

By far the most significant source of young man Thoreau's humiliating shame, however, emanated from his relationship with Emerson, whom he met in 1837, the year he graduated from Harvard.

As noted earlier, Emerson had a celebrity's charisma as well as the deep learning and questioning mind befitting an independent philosopher. (He would quit the Unitarian ministry in the 1830s.) Emerson's home in Concord was the meeting-place of a "circle" or club of inquiring intellectuals, and his young friend Thoreau promptly became a regular in the household. Emerson got Thoreau started on what would be a three-million-word journal; had his writings printed in the transcendentalist publication the *Dial*; and took daily walks with his protégé, sharing ideas about books, friendship, nature, and life.

Unconsciously, Thoreau began imitating his renowned mentor (as we have seen in Chapter 1), adopting his style of walking, talking, and dressing. The unwitting mimicry was brought to public attention by James Russell Lowell in an anonymously published literary satire (1848):

> He follows as close as a stick to a rocket
> Fingers exploring the prophet's each pocket.
> Fie, for *shame*, brother bard, with good fruit of your own
> Can't you let neighbor Emerson's orchard alone?[7]

This accusation of literary pickpocketing would have had to be mortifying.

The way to overcome the "as-if" mimicry was to become his own man—relocate to Walden Pond, and "live deliberately," as Thoreau explains in *Walden:*

> I went to the woods because I wished to live deliberately, to front only the essential facts of life, and see if I could not learn what it had to teach, and not, when I came to die, to discover that I had not lived. I did not wish to live what was not life, living is so dear; nor did I wish to practice resignation, unless it was quite necessary. I wanted to live deep and suck out all the marrow of life.[8]

"Mean and Skulking . . . One Step to Suicide"

Thoreau, an abolitionist, had given considerable thought to the problem of slavery in the United States; to the Mexican-American War, which he believed was being waged to acquire territory for slaveholders; and to society's expectation that, as a citizen, he was expected to pay taxes which would support such enterprises.

One day late in July 1846, during his sojourn at Walden Pond, the twenty-nine-year-old poet-naturalist walked through the streets of Concord, Massachusetts, to pick up a mended shoe at the cobbler's. On his way, he encountered Sam Staples, the tax collector, jail keeper, and constable, whom he knew.

Staples asked Thoreau when he was going to pay his poll tax. Thoreau had ignored doing so for six years. Since they were friends, Staples offered to pay it himself if Henry was "hard up," but Thoreau said it was a matter of principle. When Staples asked if there was nothing he could do to avoid imprisoning him, Thoreau suggested he could quit his job, which Staples was disinclined to do.

Thoreau was now in a bind. Prison was a scandalous place, even if Thoreau's incarceration was a matter of principle, as had recently been the case with his friend Bronson Alcott and another early tax resister, Charles Lane. It could be a life-changing step and undoubtedly stressful. However, Thoreau was prepared to go to jail, having received several prior warnings, and when Staples said he'd have to lock him up "pretty soon," after a moment's deliberation Thoreau responded, "As well now as any time, Sam."[9]

The next day a family member (probably an aunt) paid the tax, and Thoreau went huckleberry-picking with friends on Fair Haven Hill, where, as he would write, "the State was nowhere to be seen."

Emerson considered his protégé's going to jail "mean and skulking, and in bad taste."[10] From the perspective of this Boston Brahmin, it lacked gentility:

The State is a poor, good beast who means the best: it means friendly. A poor cow who does well by you,—do not grudge it its hay. . . . As long as the State means you well, do not refuse it your pistareen [a small coin used in the United States in the eighteenth century]. . . . The prison is one step to suicide.[11]

It was not Thoreau's perception that the State was a "good beast who means the best," but rather "a government which imprisons unjustly." Consequently, he refused it his coin of the realm and after release gave a talk about conscientious objection at the Concord Lyceum, "The Relation of the Individual to the State," which was published under the title "Resistance to Civil Government" (1849) and republished as "Civil Disobedience" in 1866. In it he wrote:

I do not care to trace the course of my dollar, if I could, till it buys a man or a musket to shoot one with,—the dollar is innocent,—but I am concerned to trace the effects of my allegiance. In fact, I quietly declare war with the State, after my fashion . . .[12]

Principled action provided the entering wedge separating Thoreau's relationship with Emerson, which had been characterized by mimicry:

Action from principle,—the perception and the performance of right,—changes things and relations. . . It not only divides states and churches, it divides families. . .[13]

Going to jail not only liberated Thoreau from psychological thralldom to his charismatic mentor, but proved to be an effective tool for social reform, affecting millions, years later, in their struggle for freedom under the leadership of King and Gandhi.

GANDHI: UNBIDDEN WORDS

Mohandas K. Gandhi (1869–1948), a major spiritual and political leader in India, was the pioneer and perfector of *satyagraha*—resistance through mass civil disobedience, which he used in the fight for *swaraj*, the independence of India from foreign domination. Gandhi's application of Thoreau's concept of civil disobedience, in turn, inspired Dr. Martin Luther King, Jr., in his struggle against Jim Crow during the bus boycott in Montgomery, Alabama, in the mid-1950s, as we shall see.

Throughout his life Gandhi struggled with feelings of shame, beginning in childhood when he stole coins from family servants to buy cigarettes. He felt mortified by these feelings, even contemplating suicide, but he lacked the courage to resolve the matter.

An episode he called his "double shame" was a different matter. His father was terminally ill and sixteen-year-old Gandhi, who had been caring for him, was one day relieved of his duties by an uncle. Going directly to his pregnant wife, he was having sexual relations with her when a servant knocked to say his father had died. Gandhi wrote:

> The shame of my carnal desire at the critical hour of my father's death, which demanded wakeful service . . . is a blot which I have never been able to efface or forget.[14]

In addition to personal shame, Gandhi was preoccupied with the problem of violence. *Ahimsa*, nonviolence, (*a*, "without," + *himsa*, "harm") was one of his basic precepts: "Non-violence is the greatest force at the disposal of mankind. It is mightier than the mightiest weapon of destruction devised by the ingenuity of man."[15]

The first time Gandhi decided to use food abstention for political leverage occurred soon after leaving the Satyagraha ashram, where he painstakingly practiced ahimsa. He was called upon to defuse a tense labor-management dispute in Ahmedabad, India's major textile-producing city, in 1916. Management refused to negotiate and Gandhi counseled the workers to strike, but insisted on several preconditions: 1) There would be no bloodshed; 2) the workers would continue to strike until management responded; and 3) the workers would seek employment elsewhere to support themselves until the end of the strike.

The workers agreed to these caveats, and upheld their commitment for two weeks, but then their morale began to flag and Gandhi felt an impending disaster—violence might break out across the picket line. Since he had called for the strike, he felt responsible for the possible ensuing bloodshed: "I felt deeply troubled and set to thinking furiously as to what my duty was in the circumstances."

Suddenly his life was transformed. He described the episode:

> One morning—it was at a mill hands' meeting—while I was still groping and unable to see my way clearly, the light came to me. Unbidden and all by themselves, the words came to my lips: "Unless the strikers rally," I declared to the meeting, "and continue the strike until a settlement is reached, or till they leave the mill altogether, I will not touch any food."[16]

Within three days the strike was settled without bloodshed, and Gandhi had discovered a modus operandi for dealing with the iron fist of British colonialism. He had pondered Thoreau's "Civil Disobedience," and put it to practice for the first time, adding to it his code of *ahimsa*, nonviolence.

KING: "STAND UP FOR RIGHTEOUSNESS, FOR JUSTICE, FOR TRUTH"

Growing up in the South, Martin Luther King, Jr. (1929–1968) was mortified by racism on a number of occasions. As a high school student, for example, after giving a thoughtful presentation, "The Negro and the U.S. Constitution," at a school located a distance from his own, he had to relinquish his seat to a white man and stand ninety minutes on the bus ride back to Montgomery, Alabama. He stated it was the angriest he had ever felt, although he suffered in silence. "Unmerited suffering is redemptive,"[17] he would one day be able to say, having experienced loathsome bigotry over the years.

The most troubling episode of his life occurred after a meeting of the Montgomery (Alabama) Improvement Association (MIA), of which King was named leader.

Rosa Parks had been arrested on December 2, 1955, for violating the city ordinance mandating segregation by refusing to leave her seat on a bus so that a white man could sit while she stood. The MIA organized a bus boycott.

From then on, King received a stream of threatening letters and telephone calls. On January 27, 1956, around midnight, he received a particularly menacing call. Upon picking up the phone he heard a voice blurt out: "Nigger, if you aren't out of this town in three days, we gonna blow out your brains and blow up the house."[18]

Downstairs in his kitchen, he pondered the problem over a cup of coffee. Married and the father of a newborn daughter, King felt he wanted to quit the MIA and leave town, but he did not want to appear cowardly. He was ashamed of his cowardly feelings and prayed:

> Oh, Lord, I'm down here trying to do what is right. But, Lord, I must confess that I'm weak now. I'm afraid. The people are looking to me for leadership, and if I stand before them without strength and courage, they too will falter. I am at the end of my powers. I have nothing left. I can't face it alone.[19]

King then felt a presence he had never before experienced (Thoreau's invisible companion comes to mind) while an inner voice seemed to say, "Martin Luther, stand up for righteousness. Stand up for justice. Stand up for truth. And lo, I will be with you, even unto the end of the world."[20]

He felt an inner calm thereafter that he had never known before, which remained with him for the rest of his life. When he learned a few days later that his home had been bombed, he returned to it with equanimity, aware that he would be able to cope no matter what the circumstances. His house was damaged, but his wife and child were unharmed.

King's father advised him to carry a gun in view of the threats and violence, quoting Ecclesiastes (9:4): "For whoever is joined with all the living, there is hope; surely a live dog is better off than a dead lion." But the son replied, "I will not stoop to the level of the oppressor."

Following the example of Gandhi, who had profoundly affected his way of thinking, King practiced and preached nonviolence, adding Christian ethics to Gandhi's Brahmanism:

> To meet hate with retaliatory hate would do nothing but intensify the existence of evil in the universe. Hate begets hate; violence begets violence; toughness begets a greater toughness. We must meet the forces of hate with the power of love; we must meet physical force with soul force.[21]

King's equanimity persisted even in the face of death, which he confronted on a regular basis until the day he stood openly facing the assembled crowd on the balcony of the Lorraine Motel in Memphis on April 4, 1968.

NOTES

1. Thoreau, *Walden*, 90–91.
2. Albert Camus, *The Myth of Sisyphus and Other Essays*, Justin O'Brien, tr. (New York: Vintage, 1955).
3. Thoreau, *Journal*, 1:34–35 (March 5, 1838).
4. Ibid., 2:101, (Nov. 16, 1850).
5. See Michael A. Sperber, *Henry David Thoreau: Cycles and Psyche* (Higganum, CT: Higganum Hill Books, 2004), 5–7.
6. Walter Harding, *The Days of Henry Thoreau*. New York: Dover, 1992, 161.
7. Walter Harding, ed., *Thoreau as Seen by his Contemporaries*. New York: Dover, 1989, 4.
8. Thoreau, *Walden*, 90–91.
9. Harding, *Days of Thoreau*, 199.
10. Ibid., 205.
11. Ibid.
12. Thoreau, "Resistance to Civil Government," 84.
13. Ibid., 72.
14. M. K. Gandhi, *An Autobiography: The Story of My Experiments With Truth*. Mahadev Desai, tr. (New York, Houghton Mifflin, 1993), 31.
15. M. K. Gandhi, *Non-Violence in Peace and War*, Ahmedabad: Navajivan Publishing House, 1948.

16. Gandhi, *Autobiography*, 430.

17. Stephen B. Oates, *Let the Trumpet Sound: The Life of Martin Luther King, Jr.* (New York: Harper & Row, 1982), 79.

18. Ibid., 88.

19. Ibid.

20. Ibid.

21. Ibid., 79.

Part III

HALLUCINATIONS AND ILLUSIONS

Chapter Twenty-Six

Introduction: The Creative Use of Alternate States of Consciousness

A hallucination, the sensory perception of an external object in its absence, may be a normal phenomenon, although it is not usually so considered. A continuum exists between ordinary, self-generated imagery and pathological hallucinations. One can imagine, for example, a cloud in the shape of a camel with the eyes closed. Normal persons are aware that this is an illusion, and the momentary apparition is not retained as an accurate perception of reality. Psychotic persons, however, may be unable to correct the misperception.

Hallucinations may accompany schizophrenia, affective disorders, epilepsy, brain tumors, and the state following the ingestion of psychotomimetic drugs such as lysergic acid diethylamide (LSD). These differ from hypnohallucinatory phenomena (sleep-related hallucinations), which may be at least partly under willful control. Dreams can be intensely vivid, supersaturated with color (and therefore indistinguishable from reality), and non-delusional.

"Oh God," bemoans Shakespeare's Hamlet, plagued by guilt, "I could be bounded in a nutshell and count myself a king of infinite space, were it not that I have bad dreams."[1]

Good dreams, fortunately, are at least as common as bad ones, but good or bad, many scientists, artists, and writers find a way of using sleep-related hallucinations creatively. Now that psychology has moved past behaviorism's elimination of consciousness as a field for investigation, the exploration of alternate states of consciousness in the new millennium promises to be psychologically revelatory. Autoscopy is a type of hallucinatory experience.

NOTE

1. *Hamlet* 1:2.

Chapter Twenty-Seven

Joseph Conrad's *The Secret Sharer* and Autoscopic Illusion

An autoscopic illusion is the external perception of one's body, which appears to an individual as though it were in a mirror. It is seen clearly, appears suddenly and without warning, and imitates the person's movements. The appearance is usually brief, and in most cases the "dislocated body image" is seen at dusk. The person usually retains a certain detached insight into the unreality of the experience and reacts with bewilderment.

In this chapter, we explore the relationship of sensory deprivation to autoscopic illusion in connection with the novella "The Secret Sharer" (1909) by Joseph Conrad (1857–1924).

The Secret Sharer takes place aboard an unnamed ship. The captain, also nameless, feels apprehensive during his first week in command of a ship with which he is unfamiliar and a crew with whom he has never before sailed.

One night, taking a walk alone on deck, he discovers a man swimming near his boat. The captain-narrator helps him aboard and learns his name is Leggatt, that he was formerly chief mate of the *Sphere,* and that he is wanted for murder. During a storm, Leggatt had knocked down and strangled a mutinous crewman. Arrested by his ship's captain, Leggatt jumped overboard and swam away.

The captain hides Leggatt from his own crew and from the searching authorities. Soon after taking Leggatt on board, the captain experiences autoscopic hallucinations. "On opening the door," he tells us, "I had a back view of my very own self looking at a chart."[1] If another should see the two of them talking, "he would think he was seeing double, or imagine himself come upon a scene of weird witchcraft; the strange captain having a quiet confabulation by the wheel with his own gray ghost."[2] With their backs to the door, "anybody bold enough to open it stealthily would have been treated to the uncanny sight of a double captain busy talking in whispers to his other self."[3]

This "dual working of my mind," he notes, "distracted me almost to the point of insanity. I was constantly watching myself, my secret self, as dependent on my actions as my own personality, sleeping in that bed behind that door which faced me as I sat at the head of the table. It was very much like being mad, only it was worse because one was aware of it."[4]

His dislocated body peers at him as if through a mysterious looking glass: "It was, in the night, as though I had been faced by my own reflection in the depths of a somber and immense mirror."[5]

ETIOLOGY OF AUTOSCOPY:
SENSORY MONOTONY AND DEPRIVATION

Several mechanisms have been postulated for autoscopy. The organic theory contends it is caused by lesions in the cerebral cortex producing false perceptions. A psychogenic explanation hypothesizes a duplication of self arising from feelings of inadequacy.[6] Others theorize that anxiety or wish fulfillment plays a role in its etiology.

Experimentally induced sensory monotony and deprivation can produce autoscopic phenomena. In one study, isolation was accomplished by placing college students on comfortable beds, in lighted cubicles, twenty-four hours a day, during which time they wore translucent goggles that transmitted diffuse light but prevented pattern vision. They also wore cardboard cuffs from below the elbow to the fingertips, permitting free joint-movement, but limited tactile perception. Auditory stimulation was limited by a partially soundproof cubicle, in which a U-shaped foam rubber pillow was provided. A continuous hum was piped in by means of earphones in the pillow, which produced fairly efficient masking noise.

More than half the subjects reported hallucinations—two of a phenomenon they found difficult to describe, saying it was as if there were two bodies side by side in the cubicle; in one case the two bodies overlapped, partly occupying the same space. Explaining his drawing of the overlapped bodies, the subject reported, "It was as if there were two of me," and he was momentarily unable to decide whether he was A or B.[7]

Sensory Monotony and Sensory Deprivation in *The Secret Sharer*

From the very opening of Conrad's tale, the sensory deprivation and monotony of the seascape is omnipresent as the captain walks the decks alone.

Sensory deprivation and sensory monotony diminish input of neurochemical transmitters to the cerebral cortex. These transmitters ground the brain perceptually to reality. In their absence, primary process cognition occurs, characterized by disorientation, fantasies, and hallucinatory activity.

This breakthrough of primary process, when it occurs, is experienced as unwilled and surprising, since the emergent material is stored relatively inaccessibly to willful utilization. The captain's startled reaction, when he first discovers Leggatt swimming in the ocean, is certainly expressive of such surprise:

> With a gasp I saw revealed to my stare a pair of feet, the long legs, a broad livid back immersed right up to the neck in a greenish cadaverous glow. One hand, awash, clutched the bottom rung of the ladder. He was complete but for the head. A headless corpse! The cigar dropped out of my gaping mouth with a tiny plop and a short hiss quite audible in the absolute stillness of all things under heaven.[8]

The Psychodynamics of Autoscopy

It is clear that the captain's autoscopy facilitated his emotional growth at a time in his life when he was under stress. If Cain and Abel are two facets of a person's psyche, it would seem that the captain incorporated Cain-like Leggatt in the course of the latter's appearance on board, which helps him to become more assertive.

When he first learns of Leggatt's reactions to an "insolent cur" aboard his former ship, the captain undoubtedly recalls his reactions to his own chief mate. (He had felt that his chief mate sneered at him, but found it difficult to assert himself and straighten the problem out.) "He appealed to me as if our experiences had been identical as our clothes." he muses, looking at somnolent Leggatt, ". . .I saw it all going on as though I were myself inside that other sleeping suit."[9] After encountering Leggatt he states: "I had felt the need of asserting myself without the loss of time. That sneering young cub got taken down a peg or two. . ."[10]

Although the captain, when he first takes Leggatt aboard, experiences an intense, almost immediate identification with him, his autoscopic phenomena remit when he learns what he needs to know to take command of his ship: "Now I had what I wanted. . . . I hardly thought of my other self, now gone from the ship. . ."[11]

NOTES

1. Joseph Conrad, *Heart of Darkness* and *The Secret Sharer*, New York: New American Library / Signet, 1997, 56.

2. Ibid., 28.

3. Ibid., 29.

4. Ibid., 36–37.

5. Ibid., 25.

6. See M. Ostow, "The metapsychology of autoscopic phenomena," *Int. J. Psycho-anal.*, 1960, 41:619–625.

7. See Bexton et al., "Effects of decreased variation in the sensory environment," *Can. J. Psychol.*, 1954, 8:70–76.

8. Conrad, *Secret Sharer*, 22–23.

9. Ibid., 26.

10. Ibid., 36.

11. Ibid., 61.

Chapter Twenty-Eight

Friedrich August Kekulé's Apparition of a Snake and the Structure of the Benzene Ring

The idea of a connection between dreaming and creativity is an old one.

Even before Joseph interpreted Pharaoh's dream of seven fat and seven lean cows, Homer described the way that Athena came to Odysseus in dreams, guiding his accomplishments. In more recent times, S. T. Coleridge wrote the poetic fragment "Kubla Khan" in an opium-induced trance, and the noted pharmacologist Otto Loewi devised an experiment on the conduction of nerve impulses, which had come to him in a dream.

Hypnohallucinatory phenomena differ from the hallucinations that accompany fever, brain tumor, intoxication, head trauma, etc. They are most often visual, quite detailed, supersaturated with color, and so vivid that they convey an overwhelming sense of reality. As in the example of Loewi, they may be used creatively to solve problems not only in science, literature, and the arts, but in the field of mental health as well.

Dreams frequently conflate hallucinations (false perceptions) with delusions (false beliefs). Hypnohallucinatory states uncouple the hallucination from the delusion and use only the former. This occurs in the hallucinations of the drowsy state just prior to falling asleep (the hypnagogic phenomenon) and the still-sleepy state immediately upon awakening (the hypnopompic phenomenon).

Creative "dreaming," the use of hypnohallucinatory phenomena constructively, is exemplified in the practices of Friedrich August Kekulé (1822–1896), the German organic chemist whose two discoveries of molecular structure each originated in recurrent hypnagogic hallucinations.

FIRST HYPNAGOGIC HALLUCINATION:
A SWIRLING DANCE ON A LONDON OMNIBUS

The first of Kekulé's two important contributions to the field was envisioned atop a London omnibus in 1855. It was a fine summer evening and Kekulé, who had been visiting a friend in Islington where he had been discussing his "beloved chemistry," was traveling to the opposite end of the metropolis on the last bus of the day. The city, usually teeming with people, was deserted. Seated alone, on the upper deck of the bus, Kekulé sank into a reverie:

> Visions of the atoms flitted before my eyes. I had always seen them in movement, those little creatures, but I had never succeeded in overhearing the secret of their movement. Today I saw that often two small ones would join to form pairs; larger ones would embrace two smaller ones, and even larger ones would seize hold of three and even four, the whole circling in a swirling round dance. I saw larger ones form a line, dragging along smaller ones at the end of the chain. . . . The conductor's cry, "Clapham Road!" awakened me from my reverie, but I spent part of the night getting at least sketches of those dreamt patterns down on paper. That was how the structural theory came to be.[1]

It is worth noting that Kekulé was so familiar with the flitting atoms from his practices that he personalized them, calling them "those little creatures." Sensory deprivation, used in the experimental induction of psychosis, is evident on this summer evening bus ride, alone through the deserted city at dusk. Kekulé's sketches of his "little creatures" led to the discovery of the linear arrangement of atoms in straight-chain compounds in which carbon is present, the carbon-chain structure theory.

SECOND HYPNAGOGIC HALLUCINATION:
A SNAKE WITH ITS TAIL IN ITS MOUTH

Kekulé's second hypnagogically inspired breakthrough in molecular theory occurred during the winter of 1861, in the elegant quarters provided him as a visiting professor at the State University of Ghent. His suite was off a narrow lane into which little sunlight entered, and on this evening, seated alone in the dark room with his back to the fireplace, he was working on his textbook of chemistry. The writing was not going well.

> My mind was preoccupied with other things. I turned my chair toward the fireplace and sank into a state between waking and sleeping (*halbschlaf*). Again

visions of atoms flitted before my eyes. This time smaller groups lingered modestly in the background. My mind's eye, sharpened by repeated visions of this sort, could now distinguish larger structures, composed in a variety of ways. Long lines, in many cases more densely fused together; everything in movement, writhing and coiling like snakes. And behold: what was this? One of the snakes seized its own tail, and the entire structure swirled mockingly before my eyes. As if in a flash of lightning I awoke; this time, too, I spent the rest of the night working out the implications of the hypothesis.[2]

As with many pursuits, Kekulé's practice made perfect: "My mind's eye, sharpened by repeated visitations of this sort, could now distinguish larger structures, composed in a variety of ways."

When his visions led him beyond the hypnagogic, into paranoia ("the entire structure swirled mockingly before my eyes"), he rapidly exited from the delusion—"as if in a flash of lightning."

Initially stymied because he had assumed benzene's six-carbon structure was linear, Kekulé's vision of a snake mouthing its tail facilitated cognitive reorganization, accomplished by using a creative type of thinking designated "homospatial process" by the psychiatric theorist Albert Rothenberg:

> Kekulé, as have other creative scientists and artists, actively conceived two discrete entities occupying the same space. He mentally superimposed an image of a snake onto images of atoms and the idea of a closed benzene ring was subsequently articulated.[3]

Rothenberg considers this a "janusian process," defined as "deliberately conceiving opposites or antitheses *simultaneously*."[4] Kekulé "saw the functionally and spatially opposite ends of the snake, tail and mouth, brought together, and he conceived them simultaneously operating in the benzene ring structure."[5]

"Highly Indiscreet Disclosures from My Inner Life"

On the twenty-fifth anniversary of Kekulé's breakthrough discovery of benzene's cyclic structure, an elaborate *Benzolfest* (Benzene festival) was held in his honor at Berlin's City Hall in 1890. Following the reading of congratulatory messages from worldwide chemical societies, Kekulé prefaced his "Fest Speech" with a rather curious comment:

> Perhaps it will interest you, if I let you know through highly indiscreet disclosures from my inner life, how I arrived at some of my ideas.[6]

The comment is curious because Kekulé presented no "highly indiscreet disclosures from [his] inner life"—at least by current standards. It must be kept in mind, however, that the majority of those in the *Benzolfest* audience—rational, work-oriented government representatives, academic scientists, and chemical industry leaders for whom Kekulé's discovery had opened profitable commercial horizons—would have found it "highly indiscreet" to "dream up" a scientific discovery. This is the most likely explanation for Kekulé's prefatory comment, although it is also possible to consider his remark from the Freudian perspective of "condensation."[7]

CREATIVE DREAMING

Dream-state hallucinations may be analogous to shuffling cards that were initially sequenced according to number and suit. Both provide a fresh start, a new deal. As the dream-researcher Wynn Schwartz writes:

> Beyond our construction of the pragmatic limits of the real world, our cognition is further limited by our rigidities, defenses, and other psychological blinders. We have our personal reasons which make it difficult for us to find or create new paradigms. The new is often hard to tolerate if it is at odds with what we already dearly hold true. But sometimes we are able to shift our outlook if we are prepared and have sufficient flexibility. Dreaming can be a part of a creative process since dream content may involve novel representations and sleep, as we know from the REM deprivation studies, can help restore the security to tolerate looking at something that challenges our conventional understandings. Sleep restores our flexibilities within our personal limits.[8]

Drawing on Kekulé's hypnagogic discoveries, it could be said that creative dreaming involves several interrelated phases: 1) a preparatory phase in which one collects as much data as possible about the subject; 2) an incubatory phase in which the data is pondered and the problems to be solved surface; 3) the hypnagogic or hypnopompic phase in which a solution is presented in symbolic form; and 4) a phase of wakeful deliberation in which the hallucination's symbolic meaning is decoded and cognitive reorganization occurs.

NOTES

1. Cited in John H. Wotiz, ed., *The Kekulé Riddle: A Challenge for Chemists and Psychologists* (Clearwater, FL, Cache River Press, 1993), 292–93. This passage translated by K. Winston.

2. Ibid., 294. This passage translated by K. Winston.

3. Ibid., 298.

4. Ibid., 303.

5. Ibid., 304.

6. Ibid., 248. This passage translated by O. J. Benfey.

7. Condensation occurs when one element in a dream's manifest content symbolizes one or more latent phenomena. The mouth-tail snake, for example, could symbolize not only the benzene ring, but the ouroboros and autofellatio. A vision of the ouroboros (Greek, "tail-devourer"), seen as early as 500 A.D. on a Mesopotamian utensil, and symbolizing infinity or eternal life, would hardly be indiscreet. On the other hand, a snake (often considered a phallic symbol), mouthing its tail, could symbolize autofellatio. We lack Kekulé's free associations to his hypnagogic image, which might also illuminate the paranoid delusion—"the entire structure swirled mockingly before my eyes." The image of autofellatio, condensed into the same symbol as the benzene ring, could explain why Kekulé considered his disclosures "highly indiscreet"; why five years elapsed after the first discovery before the second occurred; and why it was revealed in the form of a dream, in which his unconscious wish could have been disguised.

8. Wotiz, op. cit., 280.

Chapter Twenty-Nine

Henry David Thoreau: An Imaginary Mountain, a Symbolic Tombstone

"I do not invent in the least," said Henry Thoreau of his hallucinated mountain, "but state exactly what I see. I can see its general outline as plainly now in my mind as that of [Mount] Wachusett."[1] Thoreau's hallucination of an enormous mountain ("in the easterly part of our town, where no high hill actually is"[2]) recurred some twenty times over the years and was quite vivid. The hallucination was visual-tactile, undoubtedly constructed from the sensory experiences of his two ascents of Wachusett at different times in his life.

In the extensive journal entry concerning his recurring dream, Thoreau lucidly describes the nature of hypnopompic hallucination:

> There are some things of which I cannot at once tell whether I have dreamed them or they are real; as if they were just, perchance, establishing, or else losing, a real basis in my world. This is especially the case in the early morning hours, when there is a gradual transition from dreams to waking thoughts. . . At least, until we have for some time changed our position from prostrate to erect, and commenced or faced some of the duties of the day, we cannot tell what we have dreamed from what we have actually experienced.[3]

Baffled by his recurrent hallucination, Thoreau sought unsuccessfully to comprehend its antecedents: "Whether anything could have reminded me of it in the middle of yesterday . . . I doubt."[4] He had, however, repressed a curious episode that occurred two days before.

Observing some "cheerless-looking, slate-colored clouds," suddenly Thoreau noted the appearance of a low-slanting beam of sunlight, which illuminated a group of gray maples. "The intensity of the light was surprising and impressive like a halo," he wrote, "a glory in which only the just deserved to live."[5] In this "serene, elysian light," Thoreau recalled his unfulfilled aspirations: "At the eleventh hour, late in the year, we have visions of the life we might have lived. . . .It was such a light as we behold but dwell not in!"[6]

Although he pondered the possible relevance of the imaginary mountain's location (above an existing cemetery in Concord), he dismissed its significance:

> It chances, now I think of it, that it rises in my mind where lies the Burying-Hill. You might go through its gate to enter the dark wood (perchance that was the grave) but that hill and its graves are so concealed and obliterated by the awful mountain that I never thought of them as underlying it."[7]

As an afterthought, Thoreau wondered about a possible connection between cemeteries and journeys that surmount the underlying graves: "Might not the graveyards of the just always be hills, ways by which we ascend and overlook the plain?"[8] The reference to "graveyards of the just" calls to mind the halo of light that Thoreau saw two days before the hallucinations, in which "only the just deserved to live."

In order to understand the latent content of the hallucination, it is essential to understand the relationship between Henry Thoreau and his beloved brother, John Thoreau, Jr., discussed earlier in this book, and to re-emphasize the impact on Henry of John's shocking, tragic death.

John, as we have seen, was an attentive brother, indeed a virtual father to Henry. They attended the same school and, after graduation, taught at the same academy. John was the most just man Henry had ever met.

When the brothers both fell in love with the same young lady, Ellen Sewall of Scituate, Massachusetts, however, their relationship was profoundly strained. Henry deferred to his older brother but surely must have wanted him out of the way to have Ellen all to himself.

When John contracted tetanus from a wound infection and died of lockjaw, sibling rivalry was conjoined with oedipal strivings and Henry's guilt must have been immense. Ten days after John's hideous death from tetanus, Henry himself developed its signs and symptoms, and although he was not physically infected, doctors were afraid he too might die.

Henry gradually recovered from facsimile lockjaw, a conversion reaction, but developed severe post-traumatic stress disorder (PTSD, discussed in earlier chapters). On anniversaries of John's death, he experienced dreadful nightmares.[9] John was Henry's ego ideal in life and remained so even after death. As the fifteenth anniversary of John's death approached, Henry wrote to Emerson's sister-in-law:

> I do not wish to see John ever again—I mean him who is dead—but that other whom only he wished to see, or to be, of whom he was the imperfect representa-

tive. For we are not what we are, nor do we treat or esteem each other for such, but for what we are capable of being.[10]

Considering the high esteem in which Henry held John, Thoreau's perceptions of the mountain's summit is less perplexing. On it, he said, he felt as if he "trod with awe the face of a god turned up, unwittingly but helplessly yielding to the laws of gravity."[11] There, Henry seemed to behold a "hard-featured god reposing, whose breath hangs about his forehead."[12] It seemed that the mountain "ever smoke[d] like an altar with its sacrifice."

One may regard the mountain, perched atop John's grave in Henry's mind, as a symbolic tombstone. If Henry wanted John out of the way to have Ellen to himself, John could be considered the altar's sacrifice. Although the pleasure of ascending and descending the imagined mountain was mixed with awe and uneasiness about his sanity, Thoreau also found the wayfaring recreational. "I keep this mountain to ride instead of a horse," he told a friend.[13]

Another reference to a horse comes to mind while pondering the one grazing in Thoreau's psyche. It is found, or rather lost, in a not readily comprehensible parable in *Walden*:

> I long ago lost a hound, a bay horse, and a turtle-dove, and am still on their trail. Many are the travelers I have spoken [with] concerning them, describing their tracks and what calls they answered to. I have met one or two who heard the hound, and the tramp of the horse, and even seen the dove disappear behind a cloud, and they seemed as anxious to recover them as if they had lost them themselves.[14]

Some critics ascribe specific referents to these symbols. The hound has been thought to stand for Ellen Sewell's younger brother (the "gentle boy" whose virtues Thoreau extolled in the homoerotic poem "Sympathy").[15] Ellen has been considered the turtle-dove; and John, the bay horse.[16] Since John meant everything to Henry, hound, horse, and dove may represent important facets of the dead brother's psyche, lost in death.

Thoreau used the hallucination to reunite with John, his ego ideal, during times when his spirit flagged. At such times he felt that he, too, was "just," that he had the right to live (despite fratricidal guilt) and was no longer banished from a light that he "beheld but dwelled not in."

On the hallucinated mountain, which "concealed and obliterated" John's grave, Henry could distance himself from fratricidal guilt. Spiritually conjoined to John, he became a "just man." In the pre-Prozac era, Thoreau's self-induced virtual ascents were not only recreational but therapeutic. Mentally surmounting depressive imaginings, he could write, "My thoughts are purified and sublimed."[17]

NOTES

1. Henry David Thoreau, *Correspondence.* Carl Bode and Walter Harding, eds. (Westport: Greenwood Press, 1974), 498. Thoreau had ascended Mount Wachusett, 29 miles west of Concord, Mass., in July 1842 and October 1854.

2. Thoreau, *Journal*, 10:141.

3. Ibid.

4. Ibid.

5. Ibid., 132–33.

6. Ibid., 133.

7. Ibid., 142–43.

8. Ibid., 143.

9. See above, Chapter 24, "Thoreau's 'Wilderness Therapy.'"

10. Thoreau, *Correspondence*, 62.

11. Thoreau, *Journal*, 10:144.

12. Ibid., 10:142–43.

13. Thoreau, *Correspondence*, 498.

14. Thoreau, *Walden*, 17.

15. Cf. Chapter 25, "The Great Deeds of Thoreau. . ."

16. Walter Harding, ed., *Walden: An Annotated Edition* (Boston: Houghton Mifflin, 1995), 327–29.

17. Thoreau, *Journal*, 10:144.

Chapter Thirty

Demonic Hallucinations and Patricidal Guilt: Dostoyevsky's Ivan Karamazov and Freud's Bavarian Artist

The demonic hallucinations of Ivan Karamazov, in Dostoyevsky's *The Brothers Karamazov,* and of Christoph Haitzmann, a seventeenth-century Bavarian artist whom Freud studied, are remarkably similar. The manifest content of a hallucination, like a dream's, is subject to interpretation, and the hallucinations of Karamazov and Haitzmann are analyzed here from psychoanalytic, Jungian, and existential perspectives.

The Brothers Karamazov is a novel about parricide. Dmitri Karamazov asks his brother Ivan to mediate in a quarrel between himself and their debauched father, Fyodor. Dmitri believes that his father cheated him out of his inheritance and is using it to induce Grushenka, the woman they both love, to marry him. Fyodor is murdered by his illegitimate son, Smerdyakov, but Dmitri is convicted of the crime on the basis of circumstantial evidence. Shortly before the trial Ivan hallucinates the Devil.

There are indications that Ivan's devil represents the half-brother, Smerdyakov. Ivan's emotional states at the time of two hallucinations are both connected to the half brother. On the first occasion Ivan was

> overcome by insufferable depression. . . . What made his depression so vexatious and irritating was that it had a kind of casual, external character—he felt that. Some person or thing seemed to be standing out somewhere, just as something will sometimes obtrude itself upon the eye. . . . it irritates and almost torments one till at last one realizes, and removes the offending object, often quite a trifling and ridiculous one—some article left about in the wrong place, a handkerchief on the floor, a book not replaced on the shelf, and so on.
>
> At last, feeling very cross and ill-humoured, Ivan arrived home, and suddenly, about fifteen paces from the garden gate, he guessed what was fretting and worrying him.

On a bench in the gateway the valet Smerdyakov was sitting. . . . at the first glance at him Ivan knew that . . . Smerdyakov was on his mind, and that it was this man that his soul loathed.[1]

Later, at the time of a second, pre-hallucinatory aura, Ivan once again experiences the presence of the half-brother:

As he entered his own room he felt something like a touch of ice on his heart, like a recollection or, more exactly, a reminder of something agonizing and revolting that was in that room now, at that moment, and had been there before. He sank wearily on his sofa. . . . At last his eyes were fastened intently on one point. Ivan smiled, but an angry flush suffused his face. . . . There was evidently something, some object, that irritated him there, worried him and tormented him.[2]

This worrisome and tormenting object turns out to be a demonic hallucination. There is other evidence suggesting that Smerdyakov is Ivan's hallucinated devil.

The hallucination occurs shortly after the half-brother reveals to him all the sordid details of the parricide, following which Ivan says, "Do you know, I am afraid that you are a dream, a phantom sitting before me." Finally, the Devil appears to Ivan at precisely the moment when Smerdyakov hangs himself.

On the other hand, Ivan's devil resembles his father far more than the half-brother,

a Russian gentleman . . . no longer young . . . wearing a brownish reefer jacket, rather shabby. . . . It looked as though the gentleman belonged to that class of idle landowners who used to flourish in the times of serfdom . . . but . . . had sunk into the position of a poor relation of the best class.

Ivan has reason to hate his father, who abandoned him and his brothers when they were children. A critic comments: "Ivan [based] his rebellion against God on the rights of children against the fathers who mistreat then, and by analogy the rights of men against the God who has mistreated them."[3]

The passage describing Ivan's depression as he prepares to leave Fyodor's house for the last time, shortly before the murder, implies that he cannot live either with or without his father:

He had often been depressed before, and there was nothing surprising at his feeling so at such a moment, when he had broken off with everything that had brought him here, and was preparing that day to make a new start and enter upon a new, unknown future. He would again be as solitary as ever, and though he had great hopes, and great—too great—expectations from life, he could not have given any definite account of his hopes, his expectations, or even his desires.

Ivan also expresses ambivalence in his confession to the court during Dmitri's trial: "Who doesn't desire his father's death?" Ivan's hatred of his father is undoubtedly related to Dostoyevsky's attitude toward his own father, considered a rather insensate man by most of Dostoyevsky's biographers. The father was murdered by his own serfs when Dostoyevsky was eighteen years old, at which time he developed epilepsy.

Ivan is considered by many to be similar, in certain respects, to Dostoyevsky himself. Dostoyevsky's biographer, E. J. Simmons, writes that Ivan is "the most absorbing character and in many respects the mental image of his creator."[4] It would perhaps be more accurate to say that the totality of the novel reflects the complexity of diverse tensions within the author's psyche. For example, Smerdyakov is the epileptic, not Ivan.

PSYCHOANALYTIC PERSPECTIVES ON IVAN KARAMAZOV'S NONFICTIONAL COUNTERPART

In Freud's view, the psychodynamics of a Smerdyakov-type seizure results from an

> identification with a dead person, either with someone who is really dead or with someone still alive whom the subject wishes dead. The latter case is the more significant. The attack then has the value of a punishment. One has wished another person dead, and now one *is* this other person and is dead oneself. At this point psychoanalytic theory brings in the assertion that for a boy this other person is usually his father and that the (epileptic) attack (which is termed hysterical) is thus a self-punishment for a death-wish against a hated father.[5]

The above passage is from a 1928 discussion of Dostoyevsky by Freud. Interestingly, Freud also described the relationship of the demonic hallucination to the father in his 1923 essay, "A Seventeenth Century Demonological Neurosis," in which he discusses the Bavarian artist, Christoph Haitzmann (1651–1700).

Haitzmann's illness is evidenced in three parts: a diary, which records his most serious afflictions; nine paintings of the hallucinations he experienced during the course of his illness; and the statements of priests who witnessed the ordeal and of those with whom he later lived until his death.

Freud relates that in 1677 the painter Haitzmann was seized with recurrent convulsions. It seems that nine years earlier, "in a state of despondency about his art and doubtful whether he could support himself, he yielded to the Devil, who had tempted him nine times, and that he gave him his bond in writing to belong to him in body and soul after a period of nine years."[6] (Haitzmann's illness is recorded in manuscript No. 14,084 of the Austrian National Library, Vienna.)

Haitzmann was taken to the shrine at Mariazell to be exorcized. After three days, Haitzmann believed that the Devil returned the bond, and he was cured. A month later, however, convulsions and hallucinations recurred. He returned to the shrine and was assisted in recovering an even earlier pact he said he had made with the Devil. Finally cured, he entered a monastic order, where he died in 1700 "peacefully and of good comfort," according to his superior there.

Apparently, Haitzmann considered he had made a pact with the Devil while suffering from melancholia following his father's death, and Freud concluded that the painter sold himself to the Devil to be free from depression: "[H]is father's death had made him lose his spirits and his capacity for work; if he could only obtain a father-substitute he might hope to regain what he had lost."[7] As evidence for his analysis, Freud pointed out that Haitzmann's first hallucination was the Devil in the form of "an elderly citizen with a brown beard, dressed in a red cloak and leaning with his right hand on a stick."[8]

Freud concluded that Haitzmann would not have become emotionally disturbed had not poverty caused him to yearn for his father's support and sustenance. After he renounced the world and became a monk, Haitzmann's material poverty came to an end, and with it his internal struggle. In his illness, Freud wrote, Haitzmann "followed the path which led from his father, by way of the Devil as a father-substitute, to the pious Fathers of the Church."[9]

CARL JUNG'S TRICKSTER ARCHETYPE

A number of parallels exist between the devils Ivan and Haitzmann hallucinated and the archetypal Trickster figure Jung described. (See the chapter "Hawthorne's 'Wakefield.'") All three are feminized males: Haitzmann's Devil has breasts; Ivan's dreams of "becoming incarnate once and for all and irrevocably in the form of some merchant's wife weighing eighteen stone, and of believing all she believes"[10]; and the Trickster's sex "is optional despite its phallic qualities; he can turn himself into a woman and bear children."[11]

The Trickster, according to Jung, possesses a curious combination of attributes: "a fondness for sly jokes, and malicious pranks; a power as a shape shifter; a dual nature: half animal, half divine; a tendency to expose himself to torture; and an approximation to the figure of a savior."[12]

Ivan's Devil is similar, describing himself as "a sort of phantom in life who has lost all beginning and end." He says he has "a kind and merry heart" and that "as I got ready to come to you I did think as a joke of appearing in the figure of a retired general who had served in the Caucasus, with a star of the Lion and the Sun on my coat." The animal part is noted by Ivan: "If you undressed him, you'd be sure to find he had a tail, long and smooth like a Danish dog's, a yard long, dun colour."[13]

Haitzmann's Devil first appears as an innocuous old man but "later on his appearance grows more and more terrifying—more mythological, one might say. He is equipped with horns, eagle's claws and bat's wings. Finally he appears in the chapel as a flying dragon."[14]

Jung noted that "from his penis [the Trickster] makes all kinds of useful plants," considering this "a reference to his original nature as a Creator, for the world is made from the body of a god."[15] Haitzmann's Devil appeared once with "a large penis ending as a serpent." In Freud's view, a penis on the Devil represented Haitzmann's feminine attitude toward the father (whom the Devil symbolized), of a desire to have children by him.

ONTOLOGY OF THE DAIMONIC IN IVAN KARAMAZOV AND CHRISTOPH HAITZMANN

As Stephen A. Diamond reminds us, Jung was referring to the medieval idea of the daemonic when he wrote, "from the psychological point of view demons are nothing other than intruders from the unconscious, spontaneous irruptions of unconscious complexes into the continuity of the conscious process."[16]

Diamond further notes that the existential psychoanalyst Rollo May invoked the ancient Grecian notion of the *daimon* in creating his concept of the *daimonic*, which he states is

> any natural function which has the power to take over the whole person. Sex and Eros, anger and rage, and the craving for power are examples. The daimonic can be either creative or destructive and is normally both. When this power goes awry, and one element usurps control over the total personality, we have "daimon possession," the traditional name through history for psychosis. The

daimonic is obviously not an entity but refers to a fundamental archetypal function of human experience, an existential reality.[17]

The daimonic, we are told, can produce either positive or negative consequences; it is seen as a normal human drive to affirm and magnify the self. Its power can be channeled into creative energy via therapy, among other vehicles.

Eudaimonism refers to the integration of opposing forces within one's being — love and hate, creativity and destructiveness, power and impotence, etc. These forces coexist in dynamic equilibrium in the eudaimonic. When any of these antithetical forces takes over the whole person that person becomes daimonic, and experiences the state of being with unusual intensity.

The *dysdaimonic's* entire personality is dominated by one or more components of the daimonic, possessed by a blind, impersonal, self-assertive push that is disconnected from consciousness.[18]

Both Ivan Karamazov and Christoph Haitzmann are dysdaimonic. They have split their feelings of love and hate toward their fathers, projecting the good. Their hallucinated Devils are rather angelic. Ivan's, for example, says, "I am good-natured. I'll come to your assistance again." Having externalized the "good" father, they are left with only his diabolical imago. Neither had integrated filial love with parricidal fantasies, and both would be considered "possessed" rather than "in possession" of their being.

THREE VIEWS OF A HALLUCINATION AND AN OVERVIEW

Freud considered Haitzmann's hallucinations restitutive, since they embodied the fantasy of a reunion with the lost object (the father): Haitzmann "was a person, therefore, who signed a bond with the Devil in order to be freed from a state of depression." Ivan Karamazov's hallucinations seem to have a similar basis. He is also lonely and alienated. Leaving his father's house just prior to the parricide, he feels depressed and isolated. The hallucinated demons of Karamazov and Haitzmann promise respite from feelings of loss and abandonment.

From a Jungian perspective, the Devil would be considered a Trickster figure, an aspect of the shadow self, that dark, shameful, inferior part of one's being considered unacceptable. The feminized Devils of Haitzmann and Karamazov may be considered unacceptable facets of self that had been externalized. The goal of Jungian analysis is to help integrate such material into the psyche so that conscious life is not governed by the unconscious.

An existentialist approach would be to explore the way the two men's hallucinations, analyzed by Freud and Jung, created obstacles to "being in the world."

Each of the three disciplines—psychoanalytic, Jungian, and existential—seeks to understand false perceptions, in contrast to the contemporary psychiatric modus operandi, which considers all hallucinations pathological and seeks to eliminate them with antipsychotic medication.

NOTES

1. Fyodor Dostoyevsky, *The Brothers Karamazov* (New York: Fairmont Classics, 1966), 240–41.

2. Ibid., 573.

3. Edward Wasiolek, *Dostoevsky: the Major Fiction* (Cambridge: M.I.T. Press, 1964), 150, 161.

4. E. J. Simmons, *Fyodor Dostoevsky* (New York: Columbia University Press, 1969), 43.

5. Sigmund Freud, "Dostoevsky and Parricide" (1928), *Complete Works,* Standard Edition, J. Strachey et al., eds., 21:182–83.

6. Freud, "A Seventeenth Century Demonological Neurosis" (1923), ibid., 19:74.

7. Ibid., 82.

8. Ibid., 85.

9. Ibid., 104.

10. Dostoyevsky, *Brothers Karamazov,* 578.

11. Carl G. Jung, "On the Psychology of the Trickster Figure," *Collected Works* (Princeton: Princeton University Press, 1968), vol. 9, pt. 1, 263.

12. Ibid., 255.

13. Dostoyevsky, *Brothers Karamazov,* 580.

14. Freud, "A Seventeenth Century Demonological Neurosis," 85.

15. Jung, "Trickster Figure," 263–64.

16. Qtd. Stephen A. Diamond, *Anger, Madness, and the Daimonic: The Psychological Genesis of Violence, Evil, and Creativity,* Albany: State University of New York Press, 1996, 64–65.

17. Qtd. ibid., 65.

18. For further discussion, see my study "The Daimonic: Freudian, Jungian and Existential Perspectives" (1975), *Journal of Analytical Psychology* 20:41–49.

Chapter Thirty-One

The Three Phantoms of Herman Melville's *Moby Dick*

Moby-Dick, the great novel by Herman Melville (1819–1891), is the psycho-spiritual autobiography of Ishmael, a young schoolteacher, who goes whaling to alleviate his feelings of depression.

Three elusive phantoms haunt his story, figuring significantly in the novel: a phantom with a supernatural hand; a phantom with a part-tattooed, part-patchwork-quilt arm; and a phantom of Hawthorne as a "Mossy Man" in a Melville daydream. The first phantom gives the novel its central theme, the second determines its outcome, and the third provides its raison d'être.

ISHMAEL'S PHANTOM HAND

Ishmael's childhood was problematic. His mother is not mentioned in the book, and his stepmother, he says, was "all the time whipping me, or sending me to bed supperless."[1]

On one occasion, as he is trying to crawl up a chimney (acting out a re-birth fantasy?), his stepmother drags him down by the legs and orders him to stay in bed until the next day as punishment. It is only 2:00 p.m. on June 21 (the longest day of the year), and Ishmael calculates that "sixteen entire hours must elapse before I could hope for a resurrection. Sixteen hours in bed!"[2]

The small of his back aches, thinking of the prolonged bed rest; it is so light outside, the sun shining in at the window; he can hear a great rattling of coaches in the streets as well as the sound of gay voices all over the house, and he feels worse and worse.

At last Ishmael gets up, dresses, goes downstairs softly in his stockinged feet, seeks out his stepmother, throws himself at her feet, and beseeches her to give him "a good slippering" for his misbehavior—anything but condemn him to lie abed for such an unendurable length of time. She refuses his request and sends him back to his room.

He lies wide awake for several hours "feeling a great deal worse than . . . ever [before] . . . even from the greatest subsequent misfortunes."[3] At last he falls into a troubled nightmare and, slowly waking from it—half steeped in dreams—opens his eyes. It is utterly dark. Nothing can be seen or heard. Instantly, he feels a shock running through him:

> A supernatural hand seemed placed in mine. My arm hung over the counterpane, and the nameless, unimaginable, silent form or phantom, to which the hand belonged, seemed closely seated by my bedside.[4]

For what seems "ages piled on ages," Ishmael lies there, frozen with the most awful fears, not daring to remove his hand, thinking that if he could move it a single inch, the horrid spell would be broken. He does not know how "this consciousness at last glided away," but waking next morning says:

> I shudderingly remembered it all, and for days and weeks and months afterwards I lost myself in confounding attempts to explain the mystery. Nay, to this very hour, I often puzzle myself with it.[5]

Just prior to falling asleep, or immediately upon awakening, many so-called normal people (as we have seen in discussing Kekulé, above) experience an altered state of consciousness called, respectively, hypnagogia or hypnopompia, in which vivid auditory, tactile, or visual hallucinations occur. Such hypnohallucinatory phenomena may be so vivid that they are difficult to distinguish from reality. Ishmael has an early-morning hypnopompic hallucination, which typically mystifies him: "Whether it was a reality or a dream, I never could entirely settle."[6]

It is clear, however, that the unsolved mystery of his hypnopompic hallucination is important to him. The reason for its significance may be intuited from Ishmael's associations to it years later, occasioned by a profoundly affecting homoerotic experience.

Before going out to sea, Ishmael spends the night at an inn, sharing the only remaining bed with Queequeg, a Polynesian harpooner. In the morning he awakens to find Queequeg's arm thrown over him in "the most loving and affectionate manner," and reflects, "You had almost thought I had been his wife."[7]

Ishmael then reports a hypnopompic illusion in which he finds Queequeg's arm and the counterpane indistinguishable:

> The counterpane was of patchwork, full of odd little parti-colored squares and triangles; and this arm of his tattooed all over with an interminable Cretan labyrinth of a figure, no two parts of which were of one precise shade—owing I suppose to his keeping his arm at sea unmethodically in sun and shade, his shirt sleeves irregularly rolled up at various times—this same arm of his, I say, looked for all the world like a strip of that same patchwork quilt. Indeed, partly lying on it as the arm did when I first awoke, I could hardly tell it from the quilt, they so blended their hues; and it was only by the sense of weight and pressure that I could tell that Queequeg was hugging me.
>   My sensations were strange.[8]

Describing these strange sensations, Ishmael has an association to the early hypnopompic hallucination: "When I was a child, I well remember a somewhat similar circumstance that befell me." On the earlier occasion he lay "frozen with the most awful fears," but this time it is entirely different, "hugging a fellow male in that matrimonial sort of style." He states, "I lay quietly eyeing him, having no serious misgivings now, and bent upon narrowly observing so curious a creature."[9]

There is a similarity between the episode of Ishmael's childhood phantom and the one with the Polynesian harpooner:

> Now, take away the awful fear, and my sensations at feeling the supernatural hand in mine were very similar, in their strangeness, to those which I experienced on waking up and seeing Queequeg's pagan arm thrown round me.[10]

It would seem that Ishmael has a need for, and a fear of, a helping hand when, in childhood, he experienced the supernatural grasp. He overcomes that fear in the trial mini-marriage to Queequeg.

On the whaling voyage, Ishmael squeezes out the lumps in rendered cetacean sperm oil until, he says, "a strange sort of insanity came over me":

> I found myself unwittingly squeezing my co-laborers' hands in it, mistaking their hands for the gentle globules. Such an abounding, affectionate, friendly, loving feeling did this avocation beget; that at last I was continually squeezing their hands, and looking up into their eyes sentimentally; as much as to say,—Oh! my dear fellow beings, why should we longer cherish any social acerbities, or know the slightest ill-humor or envy! Come; let us squeeze hands all round;

nay, let us all squeeze ourselves into each other; let us squeeze ourselves universally into the very milk and sperm of kindness.[11]

The passage, reminiscent of Walt Whitman's "universal democratic comradeship," is the third in a sequence of events, preceded by two hypnopompic hallucinations. Each event involves Ishmael in intimate contact with real or imagined hands or arms, which leads him to conclude, "No more my splintered heart and maddened hand were turned against the wolfish world." Ahab, contrariwise, stands immobile, his peg leg anchored in a "stand-point," an auger hole bored into the deck to keep him steady in a gale.

AHAB'S PHANTOM LIMB

The sensation of a limb being present in its absence, called the phantom-limb phenomenon, results from the stimulation of nerves that originally carried impulses from the missing limb and continue to send impulses to the brain.

The pain that a phantom limb may generate may be excruciating, intractable, chronic, and almost impossible to treat; is variously described as burning, aching, or "as if the hand were being crushed in a vice," etc. There is evidence for altered nervous activity within the brain as a result of the loss of sensory input from the amputated limb. The development of phantom pain is correlated with changes in the way peripheral areas of the body are represented in the sensory cortex.

Phantom-limb pain from the stump of the leg of Ahab, which was amputated by the white whale, triggers his reactive psychosis, according to Captain Peleg, an owner of the *Pequod*:

On the passage home, he was a little out of his mind for a spell; but it was the sharp shooting pains in his bleeding stump that brought that about. I know too that ever since he lost his leg last voyage by that accursed whale, he's been a kind of moody—desperate moody, and savage sometimes.[12]

Ishmael further elaborates:

It is not probable that this monomania in him took its instant rise at the precise time of his bodily dismemberment. . . . he probably but felt the agonizing bodily laceration, but nothing more. Yet, when by this collision forced to turn towards home, and for long months of days and weeks, Ahab and anguish lay stretched together in one hammock, rounding in mid winter that dreary, howling Patagonian

Cape; then it was, that his torn body and gashed soul bled into one another; and so interfusing, made him mad.[13]

Ahab, too distracted by his wound and its sequelae (he was apparently castrated by the slippage of a whalebone prosthesis) to find intimate kinship, does not squeeze, like Ishmael, but "splices hands" in a vengeful pact with his crew to "dismember his dismemberer." The extent of his vindictiveness is an enigma even to himself:

> What is it, what nameless, inscrutable, earthly thing is it; what cozening, hidden lord and master, and cruel, remorseless emperor commands me; that against all natural loving and longings, I so keep pushing, and crowding, and jamming myself on all the time; recklessly making me ready to do what in my own proper, natural heart, I durst not so much as dare.[14]

The fashioning of a new limb does not erase the shadow of the old one. Ahab strives to disconnect himself totally from every trace of the old leg, but the existence of the phantom limb does not allow him to forget it. The fleshly counterpart travels with him as he journeys toward the unattainable white whale, to whom his last words are addressed:

> Towards thee I roll, thou all-destroying but unconquering whale; to the last I grapple with thee; from hell's heart I stab at thee; for hate's sake I spit my last breath at thee.[15]

The maimed captain, obsessed that he has been "dismasted," throws the harpoon at the "dismemberer" but the rope winds around his neck. Attached by it to the whale, who jolts forward, he is shot out of the boat, fatally smites the sea, and disappears into its unfathomable depths.

MELVILLE'S "MOSSY-MAN" PHANTOM

Herman Melville first met Nathaniel Hawthorne in early August 1850 (some three months before the publication of *Moby-Dick*), and by the end of that month Melville had bought a home in the Berkshires, six miles from Hawthorne, relocating to it from New York in the fall. The intensity of his feelings resulted from a number of factors. Melville's father died when he was thirteen, and perhaps he saw in Hawthorne, who was fifteen years older, a father figure. Both had in common a love of solitude and the sea. Perhaps Melville was also attracted to Hawthorne's "pretty-boy" good looks and found him comely.

Until Melville met Hawthorne, he had written adventure stories. The symbols that Hawthorne used in "The Birthmark" and "The Minister's Black Veil" captured his imagination; the greatness of his book about a white whale resides in its symbolism, incorporated after meeting Hawthorne.

From Hawthorne's perspective, both Melville and his own father were sailors. As we saw in the chapter "Hawthorne's 'Wakefield,'" Captain Hathorne never returned from his voyage in 1808, when his son was four years old. (He died of yellow fever in Dutch Guyana.) Perhaps Hawthorne feared abandonment by another man of the sea.

Much of what transpired between them is conjectural since only Melville's letters to Hawthorne remain, whereas the Hawthorne-Melville letters have been destroyed.

Some clues about the Hawthorne-Melville relationship do, however, exist. It would seem that Melville had a homoerotic fantasy about Nathaniel that did not correspond with the predilections of his "closeted" friend. Thus, in a review of *Mosses from an Old Manse* (written in the guise of a Virginian vacationing in New England) Melville muses:

> Stretched on that new mown clover, the hill-side breeze blowing over me through the wide barn door, and soothed by the hum of bees in the meadows around, how magically stole over me this Mossy Man. . . The soft ravishments of the man spun me round about in a web of dreams. . . .
>
> Already I feel that this Hawthorne has dropped germanous seeds into my soul. He expands and deepens down, the more I contemplate him; and further and further, shoots his strong New England roots in the hot soil of my Southern soul.[16]

After receiving Hawthorne's letter with his responses to *Moby-Dick* (which Melville dedicated to him), Melville wrote him:

> In me divine magnanimities are spontaneous—catch them if you can. The world goes round, and the other side comes up. So now I can't write what I felt. But I felt pantheistic then—your heart beats in my ribs and mine in yours, and both in God's.[17]

Since Hawthorne was the man of his dreams, and he "spun round about in their web," Melville's view of him was determined by unconscious factors. The more so, since his Mossy Man (someone who could cover him like a ground covering) was rather closeted, not unlike the Rev. Mr. Dimmesdale, protagonist of "The Minister's Black Veil." Hawthorne built his personality, as he states he built his fiction, on the "territory, somewhere between the real world and fairy-land, where the Actual and the Imaginary may meet, and each imbue itself with the nature of the other."[18]

Hawthorne has been described as "a fastidious man who depended on regulation—regular living, regular loving, rituals of predictable routine . . . [who] wanted a life of pattern, order, comfort."[19] Writing in *The House of the Seven Gables*, Hawthorne states: "Persons who have wandered, or been expelled, out of the common track of things, even were it for a better system, desire nothing so much as to be led back."[20]

Melville's characterization of him as the "Mossy Man" is indicative that the phantom he had conjured up totally missed the mark. The author of "The Minister's Black Veil" may have been subconsciously interested in same-sex relationships, but he was totally unprepared for Melville's frank eroticism. A year after Melville relocated to western Massachusetts to be closer to him, Hawthorne moved to Newton, in eastern Massachusetts, perhaps in a homosexual panic. Melville struggled with this rejection to the end of his life.

On some level Melville must have been aware that his expansive eroticism would have been unsettling. In a letter to Hawthorne he had written: "There is the grand truth about Nathaniel Hawthorne. He says NO! in thunder; but the devil himself cannot make him say yes."[21] Could Melville's phantom of "mossy" Hawthorne have kept alive his fantasies of the naysayer, the optimism of Ishmael learned from his relationship with Queequeg?

Although he dedicated *Moby-Dick* to Hawthorne "in token of my admiration for his genius" in 1851, "Monody," which he wrote on the death of his friend in 1864, expresses a lack of the fulfillment that Melville craved:

> To have known him, to have loved him
> After loneness long;
> And then to be estranged in life,
> And neither in the wrong;
> And now for death to set his seal—
> Ease me, a little ease, my song!
>
> By wintry hills his hermit-mound
> The sheeted snow-drifts drape,
> And houseless there the snow-bird flits
> Beneath the fir-trees' crape:
> Glazed now with ice the cloistral vine
> That hid the shyest grape.[22]

TWO PHANTOMS' DIVERGENT PATHS

The intensity of Ishmael's depression at the onset of the novel is difficult to assess because he couches it in mock-heroic, jocular banter: "This is my substitute for pistol and ball. With a philosophical flourish Cato throws himself upon his sword; I quietly take to the ship."[23]

This passage refers to Cato of Utica (95–46 BC), who, having been vanquished by Caesar during the battle at Thapsus, chose to take his own life and die a stoic death. According to Plutarch, Cato's body was found "weltering in his blood, a great part of his bowels out of his body."[24]

Unlike Cato, Ishmael inclines to externalize his melancholy:

Whenever I find myself growing grim about the mouth . . . whenever I find myself involuntarily pausing before coffin warehouses, and bringing up the rear of every funeral I meet; and especially when my hypos get such an upper hand of me, that it requires a strong moral principle to prevent me from deliberately stepping into the street, and methodically knocking people's hats off—then, I account it high time to get to sea as soon as I can.[25]

The central theme of *Moby Dick* is, according to one commentator,

[the] implicit contrast between the transfigured Ishmael, whose consciousness has been diffused into a promiscuous taste for all experience, and the wracked captain of "fiery eyes" who refused all distraction from his crusade.[26]

The first two phantoms, the frightening supernatural hand and the welcoming tattooed hugging arm, appear to be important forces guiding their beholders in formative directions and intensifying the contrast between them.

The Biblical Ishmael was born to a slave, Hagar, because Abraham believed his wife Sarah was infertile. When God granted her a son, Isaac, Ishmael and Hagar were turned out of Abraham's household. The name *Ishmael* has come to symbolize "orphan" and "social outcast."

In the first paragraph of the novel, we learn that when Ishmael gets depressed and feels as suicidal as Cato, then instead of picking fights with passing strangers, he goes to sea as soon as he can. The Biblical Ishmael's prophecy seems to fit: "He shall be a wild ass of a man with his hand against everyone, and everyone's hand against him." (Gen. 6:12)

During his relationship with Queequeg, an inner "melting" occurs: "No more my splintered heart and maddened hand were turned against the wolfish world. This soothing savage had redeemed it."[27] Resulting from the bond with his "inseparable twin brother," Ishmael has a vision of universal love while squeezing himself into "the very milk and sperm of kindness."[28]

Moby-Dick takes its form from the encounter of Ishmael, the outcast who comes to embrace universal love, and the wracked captain with "fiery eyes" in a "quenchless feud." Ishmael's fate differs radically from that of Ahab, who drowns, and that of Ahab's ship, the *Pequod*, which is drawn downward by concentric circles of a vortex that carry its small chip out of sight. Ishmael alone, supported by Queequeg's coffin life-buoy, escapes "to tell the tale."

The progression of Ishmael's phantoms led to his widening embrace. First, the "supernatural hand seemed placed in [his]," then a tattooed arm that "looked for all the world like a strip of [the] patchwork quilt" seemed to be hugging him. He remarks, "How elastic our stiff prejudices grow when love once comes to bend them."[29] Ahab's experiences are distinctly different. At first "dismantled" by the white whale, a "monomania" leads him to destruction on a hell-bent quest.

At the start of the novel, Ishmael's "hypos" (colloquial for depression) have almost gotten an "upper hand." By the end of *Moby Dick*, the "maddened hand" of the "wild ass of a man" is no longer "turned against the wolfish world."

NOTES

1. Herman Melville, *Moby-Dick* (New York; Penguin Classics, 2003), 28.
2. Ibid.
3. Ibid., 29.
4. Ibid.
5. Ibid.
6. Ibid.
7. Ibid., 28.
8. Ibid.
9. Ibid., 30.
10. Ibid., 29.
11. Ibid., 456.
12. Ibid., 89.
13. Ibid., 200.
14. Ibid., 592.
15. Ibid., 623.
16. Melville, "Hawthorne and His Mosses," in John L. Idol, Jr. and Buford Jones, ed., *Nathaniel Hawthorne: the Contemporary Reviews*. (New York: Cambridge University Press, 1994), 107–08.
17. L. Person, "The Scarlet Reader: Newton Arvin on Hawthorne and Melville," *Hawthorne in Salem* website, www.hawthorneinsalem.org/page/10226/—Accessed Mar. 31, 2009.
18. Nathaniel Hawthorne, *The Scarlet Letter*. 1850.
19. Brenda Wineapple, *Hawthorne: A Life*. New York: Random House, 2003, 228.
20. Nathaniel Hawthorne, *The House of the Seven Gables*, New York: Macmillan, 1911, 119.

21. Michael J. Davey, *A Routledge Literary Sourcebook on Herman Melville's Moby-Dick*, Routledge: 2004, 50.

22. Melville, *John Marr and Other Poems*, The Literature Network website, www .online-literature.com/melville/john-marr/24/—Accessed Mar. 21, 2009.

23. Melville, *Moby-Dick*, 3.

24. Plutarch, *Cato the Younger*, Ancient Greek Online Library website, www.greek texts.com/library/Plutarch/Cato_The_Younger/eng/328.html—Accessed Mar. 31, 2009.

25. Melville, *Moby-Dick,* 3.

26. A. Delbanco, "Introduction," ibid., xviii.

27. Ibid., 57.

28. Ibid., 456.

29. Ibid., 60.

Part IV

MOOD IMAGERY IN LITERATURE

Chapter Thirty-Two

Introduction: Icarus, Daedalus, and Bipolar Disorder

"The wisdom of some of those Greek fables is remarkable. They are the skeletons of still older and more universal truths than any whose flesh and blood they are for the time made to wear."[1]

—Thoreau, *Journal*

Awareness of the imagery associated with the fables of Icarus and Daedalus in Greek mythology, it seems to me, facilitates the detection and monitoring of mania, depression, and bipolar disorder.

According to mythology, Daedalus, an architect and inventor, is exiled for the attempted murder of his talented nephew, Perdix, while in a jealous rage. He is banished from Athens with his son, Icarus, and travels to Crete, where he builds a labyrinth for King Minos to contain the Minotaur, a flesh-eating, bull-headed man, the offspring of a union between Queen Pasiphae and the Cretan bull.

After Daedalus completes the project, King Minos imprisons him and his son in a high tower. Constructing wings of feathers and wax by which to escape, Daedalus admonishes his son to "keep at a moderate height, for if you fly too low the damp will clog your wings and if too high the heat will melt them. Keep near me and you will be safe."[2]

The youth, entranced by flying, floating, the dizzying heights, and the blazing sun, does not heed his father's guidance, but soars ever higher. When the heat melts his wings, he plummets into the sea and drowns.

These two Greek mythological figures serve to delineate personality types.

THE ICARUS COMPLEX: MANIA

The Icarus complex, delineated in 1955 by Henry A. Murray, the Harvard psychologist known for devising the widely used Thematic Apperception Test—the same professor whom we met in our chapter on the Unabomber—is comprised of a number of interrelated personality traits including the following: *ascensionism*, a love of flying, floating, heights, birds, and mountains; *narcissism*, a great craving for attention and admiration; *a fascination with fire* and *solar imagery*; *a predilection for water*, including the coast, swimming, boating, etc.; and *original imaginings* that seem far-fetched.

THE DAEDALUS COMPLEX: DEPRESSION

The Daedalus complex, which I delineate in this book's final chapter using Henry Thoreau as an example, is complementary to the Icarus complex and is based on the corresponding Greek mythological figure. It includes the following personality traits: *a preference for subterranean spaces*, such as swamps, grottoes, and caves; *a genius for invention, construction, and design*; *a delight in intricate structures,* such as labyrinths, mazes, spirals, and loops; *a depressive tendency*; *a need to dominate*; and *jealous feelings*.

The tendency of some individuals to go back and forth between these two states is more conventionally referred to as "manic depression" or "bipolar disorder," a condition we shall explore further in the next two chapters.

NOTES

1. Thoreau, *Journal*, 1:391–92.
2. Thomas Bulfinch, *Bulfinch's Mythology*, Kessinger Publishing, 2004, 105.

Chapter Thirty-Three

Manic-Depressive Mood Swings in Albert Camus' *The Fall*

The Fall, a novel by Albert Camus (1913–1960), is the five-day monologue of a guilt-ridden manic depressive. In it, the protagonist, Jean-Baptiste Clamence, reflects on his life as a wealthy, duplicitous Parisian lawyer, and on his mental breakdown, exploring his conscience and the absence of meaning in his life.

The novel is an indictment not only of Clamence, but of contemporary human society, a purpose made clear by the epigraph from the Russian novelist Mikhail Lermontov: "[It is] a portrait, but not of an individual; it is the aggregate of the vices of our whole generation in their fullest expression."

Formerly a successful Parisian lawyer, the public defender of widows and orphans, Clamence now lives an inauthentic life, is basically indifferent to the plight of others, and behaves like a libertine. His breakdown has been consequent upon an act of moral turpitude, he tells us. One evening, after departing from a tryst with his mistress, he passes a woman in black on the Pont Royal who jumps or falls into the Seine. He does not come to her rescue, telling himself that the water is too cold.

A few years after this incident, Clamence develops major depression with auditory and visual hallucinations. He relocates to Amsterdam, becomes a habitué of the Mexico City Café, and devises the complex role of "judge-penitent" to cope with his guilt and despair.

The imagery Clamence uses before and after the fall of the woman in black differs vastly. The present chapter correlates the early (Icarian) pre-fall imagery with his mania and the later (Daedalian) imagery with his depression.

THE TWO FALLS IN *THE FALL*

Clamence describes the first of the two falls halfway through the novel:

> I was returning to the Left Bank [of the Seine] and my home by way of the Pont Royal. It was an hour past midnight, a fine rain was falling. . . . I had just left a mistress, who was surely already asleep. I was enjoying that walk, a little numbed, my body calmed and irrigated by a flow of blood gentle as the falling rain.[1]

On the bridge, Clamence passes a slim young woman dressed in black who is leaning over the rail and seems to be staring at the river. He is stirred by the back of her neck, cool and damp between her dark hair and coat collar, but goes on a few moments later. After walking some fifty yards, he hears the sound of a body striking water. Despite the distance, it is dreadfully loud. He stops short, but does not turn around.

Almost at once he hears a cry, repeated several times, going downstream, which suddenly ceases. He wants to run to the rescue but doesn't move, explaining:

> I was trembling, I believe from cold and shock. I told myself that I had to be quick and I felt an irresistible weakness steal over me. I have forgotten what I thought then. "Too late, too far . . ." or something of the sort. I was still listening as I stood motionless. Then, slowly in the rain, I went away. I informed no one.[2]

Clamence never learns the fate of the woman. He does not read the newspapers over the next few days. Two or three years later, he hallucinates hearing the laughter of a woman.

Prior to the woman's fall, many of Clamence's high-flying traits, which Murray describes in persons having the Icarus complex, are evident, as noted below.

THE ICARUS COMPLEX: THE IMAGERY OF MANIA

Clamence's predilection for heights is evident. Perhaps it is a defense, to distance himself against the guilt of his earthy existence. In a long-winded monologue to a fellow habitué at the Mexico City Café he states:

> I have never felt comfortable except in lofty places. Even in the details of daily life, I needed to feel *above*. I preferred the bus to the subway, open carriages to

taxis, terraces to closed-in places. An enthusiast for sport planes in which one's head is in the open, on boats I was the eternal pacer of the top deck. In the mountains I used to flee the deep valleys for the passes and plateaus; I was the man of the mesas at least. If fate had forced me to choose between work at a lathe or as a roofer, don't worry, I'd have chosen the roofs and become acquainted with dizziness.[3]

Unlike Daedalians:

Coalbins, ships' holds, undergrounds, grottoes, pits were repulsive to me. I had even developed a special loathing for speleologists, who had the nerve to fill the front page of our newspapers, and whose records nauseated me. Striving to reach elevation minus eight hundred at the risk of getting one's head caught in a rocky funnel (a siphon, as those fools say!) seemed to me the exploit of perverted or traumatized characters. There was something criminal underlying it.[4]

His yearning for *social ascension*, the wish to achieve a spectacular rise in social status, was gratified before his fall: "I literally soared for a period of years."[5] "Living aloft is still the only way of being seen and hailed by the largest number."[6]

A Narcissist's Narcissist

Murray uses the term "cynosural narcissism," which is broader and more extreme than simple narcissism, to denote a craving for unsolicited attention and admiration, a desire to attract and enchant all eyes, just as the entire heavens revolve about the North Star ("Cynosure"). The Icarian's wish is that his mere appearance (*cynosural presence*), some startling exploit (*cynosural act*), or some moving or memorable pronouncement (*cynosural statement*) will draw all eyes.

Being a lawyer allowed Clamence cynosural presence: "My profession satisfied most happily that vocation for summits. . . . It set me above the judge whom I judged in turn, above the defendant whom I forced to gratitude."[7]

By defending criminals he felt his own fame increase through cynosural acts and statements, since the criminals had achieved a degree of notoriety that allowed him the opportunity to become famous by defending them. His need for cynosural presence is evident: "I have to admit it humbly, *mon cher compatriote*, I was always bursting with vanity. I, I, I is the refrain of my whole life, which could be heard in everything I said. I could never talk without boasting."[8]

Clamence's narcissism is evident: "My emotional impulses always turn toward me, my feelings of pity concern me. It is not true, after all, that I never loved. I conceived at least one great love in my life, of which I was always the object."[9]

Fascination with Fire and Water

Freud once called attention to the close relationship between fire and water:

> It is as if primitive man had the impulse, when he came in contact with fire, to gratify an infantile pleasure in respect to it and put it out with a stream of urine. Whoever was the first to deny himself this pleasure and spare the fire was able to take it with him. This great cultural victory was thus a reward for refraining from gratification of an instinct.[10]

Freud also noted a relationship between fire, "burning" ambition, exhibitionism, and voyeurism.

Clamence expresses the association of corporeal ascensionism with fire and water images with statements such as the following:

> A natural balcony fifteen hundred feet above a sea still visible bathed in sunlight . . . was the place where I could breathe most freely. . ."[11]

> "What I like most in the world is Sicily, you see, and especially from the top of Etna, in the sunlight, provided I dominate the island and the sea. . . . I like all islands. It is easier to dominate them."[12]

> "I could readily understand why sermons, decisive preachings, and fire miracles took place on accessible heights.[13]

> "At every hour of the day, within myself and others, I would scale the heights and light conspicuous fires, and a joyful greeting would rise toward me.[14]

Unusual, Original, and Expansive Imaginings

Describing the Icarian mind, Murray writes: "It turns readily and flexibly to imaginings which are generally, in some respects, unusual, original, surprising, childlike, farfetched, expansive or bizarre."[15] Clamence's "I would scale the heights and light conspicuous fires" falls into this category. So does his statement, "I felt like a king's son or a burning bush."[16] When Clamence explains the reason he knows he has no friends, his self-destructive imaginings are once again bizarre:

> I have no more friends. . . . How do I know I have no friends? It's very easy: I discovered it the day I thought of killing myself to play a trick on them, to

punish them, in a way. But punish whom? Some would be surprised, and no one would feel punished. I realized I had no friends. . . . If I had been able to commit suicide and then see their reaction . . . the game would have been worth the candle. But the earth is dark, *cher ami*, the coffin thick, and the shroud opaque.[17]

THE DAEDALUS COMPLEX: DYSTHYMIA AND DEPRESSION

The Need to Dominate and a "Strange Aching"

Albeit a creative genius (he has been called "the divine architect"), the mythical Daedalus was also a jealous man. His sister placed her son Perdix in his care to teach him mechanical arts. He was an apt student and one day, while walking on the seashore, he picked up the spine of a fish and copied it in iron that he notched on the edge, thereby inventing the saw. Putting two rods of iron together, he connected them at one end with a rivet and by so doing made a pair of compasses.

Envious of his nephew's accomplishments, Daedalus pushed Perdix off a high tower. Minerva, who favors ingenuity, saw him falling, changed him into a bird, and gave it his name, "partridge," *perdix* in Latin. (The partridge does not build its nest in trees or lofty places but nests in hedges, avoiding heights.) As noted earlier, Daedalus was banished from Athens because of his murderous attempt, and with his son Icarus fled to Crete.

Whereas the partridge, in its avian transformation, avoids heights, Icarus exulted in them, perhaps to elude the clutches of a homicidally jealous father. After his son's death by drowning, Daedalus became depressed, made an offering of his wings to Apollo, and vowed never to fly again.

After the fall, not of his son but of the woman in black, Clamence, once high-flying, also makes a vow:

> I never cross a bridge at night. It's the result of a vow. . . . Suppose, after all, that someone should jump in the water. One of two things—either you do likewise to fish him out and, in cold weather, you run a risk! Or you forsake him there and suppressed dives sometimes leave one strangely aching.[18]

Clamence's "strange aching" takes the form of delayed-onset chronic auditory hallucinations:

> I was aboard an ocean liner—on the upper deck, of course. Suddenly, far off at sea, I perceived a black speck on the steel-gray ocean . . . one of those bits of refuse that ships leave behind them. . . . I had not been able to endure watching it; for I had thought at once of a drowning person. Then I realized, calmly as you

resign yourself to an idea the truth of which you have long known, that that cry which had sounded over the Seine behind me years before had never ceased, carried by the river to the waters of the Channel, to travel throughout the world, across the limitless expanse of the ocean, and that it had waited for me there until the day I had encountered it. I realized likewise that it would continue to await me on seas and rivers, everywhere, in short, where lies the bitter water of my baptism.[19]

Clamence acknowledges his deceitfulness: "I have accepted duplicity instead of being upset about it."[20] Duplicity is evident in his twofold role as "judge-penitent"; the "king's son or burning bush"; and "a double face, a charming Janus."[21] Further, Clamence identifies himself on his calling card as "play actor," a role that is evident in his dealings with widows and orphans, for whom he cares very little.

The Little Ease: Life on the Diagonal

When Clamence's mood shifts from mania to depression, he enters a mental jail analogously to those imprisoned in the Middle Ages in a dungeon called the "little ease," neither high enough in which to stand nor wide enough in which to lie down. One had to live on the diagonal, which induces a hunchback mentality, especially repugnant to Clamence who asks, "Can you imagine in that cell a frequenter of summits and upper decks?"[22]

In order to circumvent the little-ease mind, he adopts the role of judge-penitent, a solution he devises that leaves him in a manic state, subject to periodic hallucinations:

Once more I have found a height to which I am the only one to climb and from which I can judge everybody. At long intervals, on a really beautiful night I occasionally hear a distant laugh.[23]

LOVE OF MAZES, LABYRINTHS, CAVES, AND THE SUBTERRANEAN LIFE

Clamence feels quite at home amidst the labyrinthine canals and passageways of Amsterdam:

Have you noticed that Amsterdam's concentric canals resemble the circles of hell? . . . you can understand then why I can say that the center of things is here.[24]

His Daedalian predilection for Amsterdam's labyrinthine passageways and fetid smells, which sets in after the woman's fall, reflects his depression:

How beautiful the canals are this evening! I like the breath of stagnant waters, the smell of dead leaves soaking in the canal and the funereal scent rising from the barges loaded with flowers.[25]

With the help of alcohol, mania, and his identification with God, Clamence staves off some of the underlying guilt and depression:

I grow taller, *très cher*, I grow taller, I breathe freely, I am on the mountain, the plain stretches before my eyes. How intoxicating to feel like God the Father and to hand out definitive testimonials of bad character and habits. I sit enthroned among my bad angels at the summit of the Dutch heaven and I watch ascending toward me, as they issue from the fogs and the water, the multitude of the Last Judgment. . . . above all, I feel at last that I am being adored![26]

The cycle is complete. As a Parisian lawyer, Clamence is in a manic state. After the fall he becomes depressed, and as the novel ends, bipolar Clamence once again becomes manic, with delusions of grandeur, engaged in the self-assumed role of "judge-penitent," confessing to a variety of guilt-provoking events to patrons of the Mexico City Café. After the confession, he holds a mirror up to another patron with whom he has struck up a dialogue, showing that person he is no better, and then he absolves them both. In this way, he defends against the guilt that has plagued him throughout the course of his inauthentic life, which began even before the woman in black drowned in the Seine.

NOTES

1. Albert Camus, *The Fall*, trans. Robin Buss (New York, Vintage, 1984), 69–70.
2. Ibid, 70.
3. Ibid, 23–24.
4. Ibid., 24.
5. Ibid, 29.
6. Ibid., 25.
7. Ibid., 49.
8. Ibid.
9. Ibid., 58.
10. Freud, "Acquisition and Control of Fire," *Complete Works*, 2:183–93.
11. Camus, *The Fall*, 24.
12. Ibid., 43.
13. Ibid., 24.
14. Ibid., 25.

15. Henry A. Murray, "Notes on the Icarus Complex," *Folia Psychiatrica, Neurologica et Neurochirurgica,* 61:42, 1958.

16. Camus, *The Fall*, 29.

17. Ibid., 73–74.

18. Ibid., 15.

19. Ibid., 108.

20. Ibid., 141.

21. Ibid., 47.

22. Ibid., 111.

23. Ibid., 142.

24. Ibid., 13.

25. Ibid., 43.

26. Ibid., 143.

Chapter Thirty-Four

Bipolar Imagery in Henry David Thoreau's Journal

From Thoreau's earliest years, episodes of suicidal depression alternated with bouts of mania: "My waking experience always has been and is . . . *Insanity and Sanity*."[1] Both affective states are evident in a number of journal passages. In the manic phase, the streams of association and flight of ideas, symptomatic of bipolar disorder, are so prominent that they can at times obscure the meaning of Thoreau's usually lucid prose.[2]

Icarian and Daedalian images appear in Thoreau's writings and drawings during the episodes of mania and depression. Icarian imagery will be discussed first.

ICARIAN THOREAU

Ascensionism is evident when Thoreau compares his mental aspirations to his physical aspirations: "My desire for knowledge is intermittent; but my desire . . . to bear my head through atmospheres and heights unknown to my feet, is perennial and constant.[3]

One of Thoreau's contemporaries described his friend's inclination to ascend mentally, spiritually, and physically:

Once, after a day so stormy that he had not taken his customary outdoor exercise, Henry came flying down from his study when the evening was half spent. His face was unusually animated; he sang with zest, but evidently needed an unrestricted outlet for his pent up vitality and soon began to dance, all by himself, spinning airily round, displaying remarkable litheness and agility; growing more and more inspired, he finally sprang over the center-table, alighting like a feather on the other side—then, not in the least out of breath, continued his waltz until his enthusiasm abated.[4]

Thoreau enjoys the sensation of floating, whether in a boat or dream, and frequently alludes to it in his writings, using the metaphor to convey the transcendental relationship between the material and spiritual realms:

This stream of events which we consent to call actual, and that other mightier stream which alone carries us with it,—what makes the difference? On the one our bodies float, and we have sympathy with it through them; on the other, our spirits.[5]

Thoreau's affinity for birds is evidenced in a quantitative study that found there are "more images in *Walden* that involve birds than of any other single phenomenon—including weather—in the whole of Thoreau's nature imagery."[6]

He compares himself to Chanticleer the rooster, who in the morning "takes his perch upon the highest rail and wakes the country with his clarion."[7] This image of the crowing cock exemplifies the connection between ascensionism and another Icarian trait discussed in this chapter, cynosural narcissism—the need to capture all eyes.

Sensing "the seasons and all their changes"[8] within himself, Thoreau feels an identity with birds in flight, particularly those in migration. At twenty-three, musing on the end of winter and the soul's final journey, he writes of (but will not "yield" to) a bodily impulse to take off:

To-day I feel the migratory instinct strong in me, and all my members and humors anticipate the breaking up of winter. If I yielded to this impulse, it would surely guide me to summer haunts. This indefinite restlessness and fluttering on the perch do, no doubt, prophesy the final migration of souls out of nature to a serene summer, . . . winging their way at evening and seeking a resting-place with loud cackling and uproar![9]

Following his brother's death on January 11, 1842, Thoreau made no journal entries for five weeks—which was quite unusual for this author, who was accustomed to journalizing almost daily. When he broke his silence, he employed the highs and lows of horizontal and vertical imagery:

My path hitherto has been like a road through a diversified country, now climbing high mountains, then descending in the lowest vales. From the summits I saw the heavens; from the vales I looked up to the heights again. . . . in adversity I remember my own elevations.[10]

The following day Thoreau expresses himself with a pure Icarian simile: "I am like a feather floating in the atmosphere; on every side is depth unfathomable."[11] Being in a manic Icarian state enables him to transcend the downside of his mood swings, corresponding with the Smooth phase of the "Rough-Smooth" anniversary dream, in which he is floating, suspended on a delicious smooth surface—"gossamer or down or softest plush."[12]

Similarly, Thoreau describes the enormous hallucinated mountain, a tombstone for John Thoreau, Jr., his ego ideal, "as if it were solidified air and cloud . . . [a] rocky, misty summit, secreted in the clouds."[13] Such a rarefied atmosphere would have smoothed his ascent to the summit.

Thoreau longs to look up to a spectacular, heroic Icarian: "What can be uglier than a country occupied by groveling, coarse, and low-lived men? No scenery will redeem it. Any landscape would be glorious to me, if I were assured that its sky was arched over a single hero."[14] That hero could be a solitary philosopher, he muses, prior to going to Walden to live:

> Whoever has had one thought quite lonely, and could contentedly digest that in solitude, knowing that none could accept it, may rise to the height of humanity, and overlook all living men as from a pinnacle.[15]

Ascension and descension are particularly evident in Thoreau's responses to love and death during the year of his involvement with the woman to whom he ultimately proposed, Ellen Sewall, during the erotically charged epoch from June 1839 to November 1840.

On June 20, 1840, for example, he writes:

> Let us remember not to strive upwards too long, but sometimes drop plumb down the other way, and wallow in meanness. From the deepest pit we may see the stars, if not the sun. Let us have presence of mind enough to sink when we can't swim. At any rate, a carcass had better lie on the bottom than float an offense to all nostrils. It will not be falling, for we shall ride wide of the earth's gravity as a star, and always be drawn upward still, . . .and so, by yielding to universal gravity, at length become fixed stars.[16]

Mild mood swings resulting from optimism and pessimism that homoerotic Thoreau, unclear about his sexual identity, may have had in working out a relationship with Ellen or her younger brother are perhaps reflected in the highs and lows of Thoreau's successive images.

Cynosural Narcissism

The Icarian trait of "cynosural narcissism" was coined from "Cynosure," the polestar, the apparent center of the rotating heavens. In this extreme form of narcissism, the individual needs to be spectacular—the star around which all the others revolve, the focus of all eyes and the center of attention. In the fore-going allusion to centrifugal force—"we shall ride wide of the earth's gravity as a star, and always be drawn upward still"—it is as if Thoreau imagines that he will be drawn upward and outward until at length he becomes a fixed star. If he can shine with stellar brightness over all humanity, he needn't be ashamed of concerns related to homo- or bi-eroticism.[17]

Fascination with Fire and Sun

Four years before summoning the resolve to move to Walden Pond, Thoreau expressed a longing for a lodge on the southern slope of some hill where, he writes, he would gratefully accept all that was his yield between sunrise and sunset:

> In the sunshine and the crowing of cocks I feel an illimitable holiness. The warm sun casts his incessant gift at my feet as I walk along, unfolding his yellow worlds.[18]

Discussing solar imagery in *Walden*, Stanley Edgar Hyman observes, "the sun is Thoreau's key symbol." *Walden* begins with the theme, "alert and healthy natures remember that the sun rose clear" and concludes with the words, "There is more day to dawn. The sun is but a morning star." Hyman argues that Thoreau's solar imagery encompasses the two extreme attitudes between which Thoreau evolved—an egocentric view ("I have, as it were, my own sun and moon and stars and a little world all to myself") and a socio-centric (actually, I would say, cosmic) view ("The same sun which ripens my beans illumines at once a system of earths like ours").[19]

An Affinity for Water

"An abundance of water imagery," according to Murray, characterizes some Icarians.[20] Thoreau's affinity for water is apparent when he writes:

> There is something more than association at the bottom of the excitement which the roar of a cataract produces. It is allied to the circulation in our veins. We have a waterfall which corresponds even to Niagara somewhere within us.[21]

Affinity with water is also evident listening to another waterfall:

> I hear the sound of Heywood's Brook falling into Fair Haven Pond, inex-pressibly refreshing to my senses. It seems to flow through my very bones.

I hear it with insatiable thirst. It allays some sandy heat in me. It affects my circulations; methinks my arteries have sympathy with it. What is it I hear but the pure waterfalls within me, in the circulation of my blood, the streams that fall into my heart? What mists do I ever see but such as hang over and rise from my blood? The sound of this gurgling water, running thus by night as by day, falls on all my dashes, fills all my buckets, overflows my float-boards, turns all the machinery of my nature, makes me a flume, a sluice-way, to the springs of nature. . . Thus I am washed; thus I drink and quench my thirst.[22]

Thoreau's major works, *A Week on the Concord and Merrimack Rivers*, *Walden*, and *Cape Cod* are structured around water—rivers, pond, and sea.

Daily bathing for Thoreau was "an undescribed luxury."[23] He writes that, when immersed in water, "I begin to inhabit the planet and see how I may be naturalized at last."[24] He compares his life to a mountain stream that "will cut its own channel . . . and will reach the sea water . . . overleaping all barriers, with rainbows announcing its victory."[25]

"Surprising, Childlike, Far-fetched, Expansive" Imaginings

Not bound to conventional ways of acting or speaking, Thoreau's unusual imaginings are often original, surprising, childlike, far-fetched, expansive, and extravagant—characteristics which (in Murray's delineation) are typical of Icarians.

Extravagance is perhaps the most characteristic element of Thoreau's style. In *Walden* he calls attention to the root meaning of this word by inserting a hyphen: *extra-vagant*, "wandering beyond":

I fear chiefly lest my expression may not be *extra-vagant* enough, may not wander far enough beyond the normal limits of my daily experience, so as to be adequate to the truth of which I have been convinced.[26]

In order to convey unconventional truths, to reveal moral and spiritual verities beneath surface appearances, to transport us unexpectedly to some higher frame of reference, Thoreau uses, as one of his modern editors, Joseph Moldenhauer, puts it, "a rhetoric of powerful exaggeration, antithesis, and incongruity" and a style that features "hyperbole, wordplay, paradox, mock-heroics, loaded questions, and the ironic manipulation of cliché, proverb and allusion." These devices are "Thoreau's means of waking his neighbors up," Moldenhauer writes. "They exasperate, provoke, tease and cajole; they are the chanticleer's call to intellectual morning."[27]

Thoreau's unconventional imagination is evident when he says:

> If by patience, if by watching, I can secure one new ray of light, can feel my-
> self elevated for an instant upon Pisgah, the world which was dead prose to me
> become living and divine, shall I not watch ever? Shall I not be a watchman
> henceforth? If by watching a whole year on the city's walls I may obtain a com-
> munication from heaven, shall I not do well to shut up my shop and turn [i.e.,
> become] a watchman?[28]

The originality of certain images is startling: "If I am well, then I see well.
The bulletins of health are twirled along my visual rays, like pasteboards on
a kite string."[29]

Sunlight and Icarian levitation are coupled in this visual association: "I am
not taken up, like Moses, upon a mountain to learn the law, but lifted up in
my seat here, in the warm sunshine and genial light."[30]

As literary critic Joseph Wood Krutch observed, the ability "to unite, without incongruity, things ordinarily thought of as incongruous *is* the phenomenon called Thoreau."[31]

DAEDALIAN THOREAU

Unlike high-flying, impulsive Icarians, Daedalians tend to have an obsessive-
compulsive personality—"scrupulous, neat, pedantic, meticulous, formal,
punctual and in ethical matters strict to the point of asceticism."[32]

Thoreau's three-million-word, fourteen-volume journal, with its punctual
almost-daily entries, meticulous measurements, scrupulous integrity, and as-
cetic morality, may attest to obsessional traits.

Such traits may be used, unconsciously, to bind anger. Like Daedalus,
who, overwhelmed by jealousy, pushed his nephew Perdix from a high place,
Daedalians may unleash homicidal rage when provoked. "My thoughts are
murder to the State and involuntarily go plotting against her," Thoreau told a
crowd in his ringing denunciation of the fugitive slave law, which was later
published as the essay "Slavery in Massachusetts." In his "Plea for Captain
John Brown," he asserted to a large audience, "I do not wish to kill or be
killed, but I can foresee circumstances in which both these things would be
by me unavoidable."[33]

In Thoreau's writings, the obsessive's fascination with anal and enteric
imagery is evident: "What have we to boast of? We are made the very sewers,
the cloacae, of nature.[34] . . . The filth about our houses . . . is quite offensive

often when the air is heavy at night. The roses in the front yard do not atone for the stink and pigsty and cow-yard and jakes in the rear."[35]

He describes the sand that was exposed by diggers for the Fitchburg Railroad near Walden Pond as "foecal and stercoral" and compares the spring thawing of this frozen clay-and-sand bank to a bowel movement, likening it to the creative process:

> So the poet's creative moment is when the frost is coming out in the spring, but, as in the case of some too easy poets, if the weather is too warm and rainy or long continued it becomes mere diarrhoea, mud and clay relaxed. The poet must not have something pass his bowels merely; that is women's poetry. He must have something pass his brain and heart and bowels, too. . . . There is no end to the fine bowels here exhibited,—heaps of liver, lights, and bowels. Have you no bowels? Nature has some bowels.[36]

Thoreau tries to steer clear of the "slimy benignity" of a certain social reformer

> with which he sought to cover you before he swallowed you and took you fairly into his bowels. It would have been far worse than the fate of Jonah. I do not wish to get any nearer to a man's bowels than usual. I do not like the men who come so near me with their bowels. . . . It is the most disagreeable kind of snare to be caught in. Men's bowels are far more slimy than their brains.[37]

Attraction to the Subterranean

Daedalians are drawn to earthy, mucky, dark places—swamps, bogs, tunnels, caves, and underground passageways. Images pertaining to sewers, swamps, and reptiles appear frequently in Thoreau's work:

> We are conscious of an animal in us, which awakens in proportion as our higher nature slumbers. It is reptile and sensual, and perhaps cannot be wholly expelled; like the worms which, even in life and health, occupy our bodies. Possibly we may withdraw from it, but never change its nature. I fear that it may enjoy a certain health of its own; that we may be well, yet not pure.[38]

Thoreau's passion for swamps when he is depressed runs throughout the journal:

> Would it not be a luxury to stand up to one's chin in some retired swamp for a whole summer's day, scenting the sweet-fern and bilberry blows, and lulled by

the minstrelsy of gnats and mosquitoes? . . . Why be eagles and thrushes always, and whip-poor-wills never?[39]

He finds swamps emotionally uplifting:

Beck Stow's Swamp! What an incredible spot to think of in town or city! When life looks sandy and barren, is reduced to its lowest terms, we have no appetite, and it has no flavor, then let me visit such a swamp as this, deep and impenetrable, where the earth quakes for a rod around you at every step, with its open water where the swallows skim and twitter . . .[40]

Desire for a Solid Grounding

With their predilection for getting bogged down and their trepidation over taking wing, Daedalians have an inordinate need for terra firma to feel mentally grounded. Thoreau expresses this early in *Walden*:

Let us settle ourselves, and work and wedge our feet downward through the mud and slush of opinion, and prejudice, and tradition, and delusion, and appearance, that alluvion which covers the globe, through Paris and London, through New York and Boston and Concord, through church and state, through poetry and philosophy and religion, till we come to a hard bottom and rocks in place, which we can call reality, and say, This is, and no mistake.[41]

Daedalian Thoreau is able to experience a similar profound satisfaction with a "rock bottom" (albeit a more squishy one) while taking a "fluvial walk" immersed in the Assabet River:

Here is a road where no dust was ever known, no intolerable drouth. Now your feet expand on a smooth sandy bottom, now contract timidly on pebbles, now slump in genial fatty mud—greasy, saponaceous—amid the pads.[42]

An Affinity for Invention, Construction, and Design

Daedalus was sometimes symbolized as the "Divine Architect" in medieval Christianity, and Daedalians are fascinated with the design and construction of buildings as well as the structure of open areas and communities.

In the first chapter of *Walden*, Thoreau expresses his view that architectural beauty gradually grows

from within outward, out of the necessities and character of the indweller, who is the only builder,—out of some unconscious truthfulness, and nobleness, without ever a thought for the appearance . . . The most interesting dwellings in this country, as the painter knows, are the most unpretending, humble log huts and cottages of the poor commonly.[43]

Thoreau's talent for *literary* architecture was noted by Ellery Channing, his walking companion and first biographer: "The impression of the *Week* and *Walden* is single, as of a living product, a perfectly jointed building, yet no more composite productions could be cited." As with these books, Channing found that Thoreau's essays "Wild Apples" and "Autumnal Tints" possess "unity of treatment" and viewed them as products of his "constructive, combining talent."[44]

Love of Circular Patterns and "Strange Loops"

Daedalians are intrigued by spirals and circles, and Thoreau's fascination with these symbols has occasioned considerable comment from scholars. As Charles Anderson wrote in *The Magic Circle of Walden*:

> Orbs, spheres, circular paths and flights, daily and seasonal cycles, orbiting stars and ripples on water—all these form an important part of Thoreau's subject matter and provide him with another way of looking at the world. The imagery ranges from insects to the cosmos and is applied to a great variety of things: animals, plants, ponds, sights, sounds, people. The very structure of his book [*Walden*] is circular, almost a Ptolemaic system of cycles and epicycles. . .[45]

Anderson cites a journal entry in which Thoreau uses circular imagery to convey his idea of the soul's centrality:

> All things, indeed, are subject to a rotary motion, either gradual and partial or rapid and complete, from the planet and solar system to the simplest shellfish and pebbles on the beach; as if all beauty resulted from an object turning on its own axis, or others turning about it. It establishes a new centre in the universe. As all curves have reference to their centres or foci, so all beauty of character has reference to the soul, and is a graceful gesture of recognition or waving of the body toward it.[46]

The circularity inherent in the walks Thoreau loved to take, as well as in "the history of his life, and even . . . in the pattern of his most characteristic prose and the structure of some of his controlling ideas," has been analyzed by Thoreau scholar John Broderick, who observes that *Walden* "might be regarded as a year-long walk, for as in his daily walk Thoreau moved away from the mundane world of the village toward one of heightened awareness and potentiality, only to return spiritually reinvigorated, so *Walden* records an adventuring on life which structurally starts from and returns to the world of quiet desperation."[47]

Thoreau's most effective writing, Broderick notes, follows the "out-and-back" movement of the "well-loved walk" or excursion. "Our voyaging is only great circle-sailing," Thoreau writes in *Walden*, while in "Walking" he affects to complain. "Our expeditions are but tours, and come round again at evening to the old hearth-side from which we set out. Half the walk is but retracing our steps." Broderick notes that "a geometric design of the life of Thoreau would run to loops and curlicues. Concord was home base for a series of forays in the larger, more or less alien world."[48]

Closely allied to a preoccupation with circles, spirals, and mazes, the Daedalian may also manifest a fascination with the "strange loop," a type of abstract structure identified by the physicist-author Douglas Hofstadter—a phenomenon occurring "whenever, by moving upwards (or downwards) through the levels of some hierarchical system, we unexpectedly find ourselves back where we started." A strange loop, he specifies, may be created in any complex structured system, "in various media and in varying degrees of richness."[49]

Discussing *Walden*, Sherman Paul points out a hidden springtime in the beginning chapter that may qualify that book's seasonal cycle as a strange loop:

> When he [Thoreau] went to the pond in March, 1845, he had already felt the influence of "the spring of springs," he had overcome his "torpidity"; . . . and had again become a "child." Though Thoreau buried this spring in "Economy," and deliberately began his account with summer, with his going to the pond to live on Independence Day, the imagery of the melting pond, the returning birds, and the stray goose were the same as in his second "spring." This additional season, of course, made it possible for Thoreau to recapitulate the entire history of his life from youth to maturity: the first spring, the dewy, pure auroral season of the Olympian life, was true to his youth, and the subsequent seasons and the second spring were the record of the growth of consciousness and of his conscious endeavor to earn the new world of his springtime again.[50]

The universe in which Thoreau felt free to construct strange loops and other forms of chutes-and-ladders was, of course, the world of words, and page after page of Thoreau's prose is replete with plays on words, double entendres, concealed meanings, and etymological short-circuits. His puns and aphorisms "tend to make their point by shifting linguistic levels."[51]

Fascination with Mazes and Labyrinths

Like other Daedalians, Thoreau was intrigued by mazes—as, for example, one he saw in snow-covered pitch pines: "It is a still white labyrinth of snowy purity, and you can look far into its recesses under the green and snowy canopy,—a labyrinth of which, perchance, a rabbit may have the clue."[52] He delighted in the wild beauty and solitude of Concord's Estabrook Country, depicting its old, irregular roads and paths as mazes:

> For my afternoon walks I have a garden . . . mile after mile of embowered walks, such as no nobleman's grounds can boast, with animals running free and wild therein as from the first,—varied with land and water prospect, and, above all, so retired that it is extremely rare that I meet a single wanderer in its mazes.[53]

Moving in his own labyrinthine circumambulations, Thoreau centered himself by sounding depths, measuring snowdrifts, and dating the tree swallow's migrations from one year to the next. With Daedalian attention to grounding facts, he transformed Concord into "the most estimable place in all the world,"[54] creating "Cosmos [order] out of Chaos."

THE IMAGERY OF MOOD—AN ARTISTIC CONSTANT?

Icarian imagery in art and literature may indicate an underlying mania, while Daedalian imagery may indicate depression. This theory, I suggested in an earlier work on Thoreau, deserves to be tested on a range of other artists.[55] Certainly in literature, as we have seen in the foregoing chapters, Camus's fallen antihero Clamence can be interpreted as a bipolar personality type, while Henry Thoreau, a historical figure, produced Icarian as well as Daedalian imagery—not only in his prose writing but also in the visual sketches he drew in his journal (birds in flight vs. concentric, inward-directed mazes such as swamplands).

Icarian imagery is unmistakable in the works of the Russian-French Jewish artist Marc Chagall, who conveyed joy and optimism with the airborne brides and bridegrooms deriving from his visions of folk culture. In contrast, the Dutch artist M. C. Escher in his lithographs and woodcuts populated mazes and impossible topographies with processions of Daedalian figures who are endlessly ascending and descending, never exiting their labyrinths.

Ancient, classic, modern and post-modern—how many more authors and artists, I wonder, invite similar investigation?

NOTES

1. Thoreau, *Journal*, 9:210–11. Thoreau's italics.
2. Cf. Michael Sperber, *Henry David Thoreau: Cycles and Psyche*. Higganum CT: Higganum Hill Books, 2004, 30–31.
3. Thoreau, *Journal*, 2:150–51.
4. Harding, *Thoreau Contemporaries*, 95.
5. Thoreau, *Journal*, 2:43.
6. Quoted in W. Harding and M. Meyers, eds., *The New Thoreau Handbook* (New York, New York University Press, 1980), 185.
7. Thoreau, *Journal*, 5:216.
8. Ibid., 10:127.
9. Ibid., 1:176.
10. Ibid., 320.
11. Ibid., 321.
12. Ibid., 9:211.
13. Ibid., 10:142.
14. Ibid., 3:23–24.
15. Ibid., 1:248.
16. Ibid., 146.
17. See Sperber, *Cycles and Psyche*, 12.
18. Thoreau, *Journal*, ed. cit., Vol. 1, 202.
19. S. E. Hyman, "Henry Thoreau in Our Time," in Sherman Paul, ed., *Thoreau: A Collection of Critical Essays* (Englewood Cliffs, Prentice-Hall, 1962), 29.
20. Henry A. Murray, "American Icarus," *Clinical Studies of Personality*, Λ. Burton and R. E. Harris, eds. (New York: Harper and Brothers, 1955), 2:639.
21. Thoreau, *Journal*, 2:155.
22. Ibid., Vol. 2:300.
23. Ibid., Vol. 4:207
24. Ibid., Vol. 6:383.
25. Ibid., Vol. 1:244–45.
26. Thoreau, *Walden*, 324. Thoreau's italics.
27. J. J. Moldenhauer, "Paradox in *Walden*," in R. Ruland, ed., *Twentieth Century Interpretations of* Walden (Englewood Cliffs, Prentice-Hall, 1968), 95.
28. Thoreau, *Journal*, 2:471.
29. Ibid., 1:266.
30. Ibid., 158.
31. J. W. Krutch, *Henry David Thoreau*, New York, Sloan Associates, 1948, 286, qtd. in Moldenhauer, 73.
32. B. Lewin, "Obsessional Neurosis," in S. Lorand, ed., *Psychoanalysis Today: Its Scope and Function* (New York, Covici-Friede, 1933), 266.
33. Thoreau, *Reform Papers*, 108, 133.
34. Thoreau, *Journal*, 2:9.
35. Ibid., 4:133.
36. Ibid., 3:165.

37. Ibid., 5:264–65.

38. Thoreau, *Walden*, 219.

39. Thoreau, *Journal*, 1:141–42.

40. Ibid., 4:231.

41. Thoreau, *Walden*, 97–98.

42. Thoreau, *Journal*, 4:220.

43. Thoreau, *Walden*, 47.

44. Ellery Channing, *Thoreau, The Poet-Naturalist* (Boston, Goodspeed, 1902), 29.

45. Charles R. Anderson, *The Magic Circle of* Walden (New York, Holt, Rinehart and Winston, 1968), 214–15.

46. Thoreau, *Journal,* 1:332.

47. John C. Broderick, "The Movement of Thoreau's Prose," in Ruland, 64, 66.

48. Ibid., 64.

49. Douglas R. Hofstadter, *Gödel, Escher, Bach: An Eternal Golden Braid* (New York: Basic Books, 1999), 10 and P7–P8.

50. Sherman Paul, ed., "Introduction," Thoreau, *Walden* and "Civil Disobedience" (Boston, Houghton Mifflin, 1960), xxix.

51. Hyman, "Thoreau in Our Time," 33.

52. Thoreau, *Journal*, 11:390.

53. Ibid., 2:38.

54. Ibid., 9:160.

55. Cf. Sperber, *Cycles and Psyche*, ch. 7–8.

Bibliography

Abagnale, Frank W., Jr. *Catch Me if You Can.* With Stan Redding. New York: Grosset & Dunlap, 1980.

Allen, Woody. *Three Films of Woody Allen: "Zelig," "Broadway Danny Rose," "The Purple Rose of Cairo."* London: Faber & Faber, 1990.

Asperger, Hans. *"Autistic Psychopathy" in Children* (1944). In Uta Frith, ed., *Autism and Asperger Syndrome.* London: Cambridge University Press, 1991, 37–92.

Barchilon, José. *"The Fall* by Albert Camus: a Psychoanalytic Study." *Int J Psychoanal.,* 1968, 49(2):386–89.

Beam, Alex. *Gracefully Insane: The Rise and Fall of America's Premier Mental Hospital.* New York: Public Affairs, 2001.

Bellin, Eva, et al. "Understanding Terrorism." *Harvard Magazine* 104 (Jan.-Feb. 2002), 36–49.

Bexton, W.H., W. Herron, and T. H. Scott. "Effects of decreased variation in the sensory environment." *Can. J. Psychol.,* 1954, 8, 70–76.

Campbell, Joseph. *The Hero with a Thousand Faces.* Princeton, Bollingen Series XVII, 2nd ed., 1968.

Camus, Albert. *The Fall.* Robin Buss, tr. London: Penguin, 2006.

———. *The Myth of Sisyphus and Other Essays.* Justin O'Brien, tr. New York: Vintage, 1955.

Carroll, Jock. *Glenn Gould: Some Portraits of the Artist as a Young Man.* Toronto: Stoddart, 1955.

Chambers, Whittaker, *Witness.* New York: Random House, 1952.

Chase, Alston. *Harvard and the Unabomber: The Education of an American Terrorist.* New York: Norton, 2003.

Chekhov, Anton. *The Portable Chekhov.* Avram Yarmolinsky, ed. and tr. New York: Penguin, 1988.

———. *Ward No. 6 and Other Stories.* David Plante, ed. Constance Garnett, tr. New York: Barnes & Noble, 2003.

Conrad, Joseph. *Heart of Darkness* and *The Secret Sharer*. New York: New American Library, 1997.

———. *Lord Jim*. Thomas C. Mosler, ed. New York: Norton, 1996.

Conrad, Randall. "Realizing Resistance: Thoreau and the First of August, 1846, at Walden." *The Concord Saunterer*, 2004–05, vol. 12/13, 165–93.

Deutsch, Helene. "Some Forms of Emotional Disturbance and Their Relationship to Schizophrenia" (1942). In *Neuroses and Character Types: Clinical Psychoanalytic Studies*. New York: International Universities Press, 1965.

Diamond, Stephen A., *Anger, Madness, and the Daimonic: The Psychological Genesis of Violence, Evil, and Creativity*. Albany: State University of New York Press, 1996.

Dostoevsky, Fyodor. *The Brothers Karamazov*. New York: Fairmont Classics, 1966.

———. *Crime and Punishment*. Sidney Monas, tr. New York: Signet, 1968.

———. *Notes from Underground*. Michael R. Katz, ed. New York: Norton, 2001.

———. *Notes from Underground, the Double and Other Stories*. New York: Barnes & Noble, 2003.

Ellmann, Richard. *James Joyce*. Oxford: Oxford University Press, 1982.

Emerson, Ralph Waldo. *Journals and Miscellaneous Notebooks*. Various editors, 16 vols. Cambridge: Harvard University Press, 1960–.

Freud, Sigmund. *Standard Edition of the Complete Works of Sigmund Freud*, James Strachey et al., eds. London: Hogart Press and Institute of Psychoanalysis, 1953–1974.

Friedrich, Otto. *Glenn Gould: A Life and Variations*. New York: Random House, 1989.

Gandhi, Mohandas K. *Gandhi An Autobiography: The Story of My Experiments With Truth*. Mahadev Desai, tr. New York, Houghton Mifflin, 1993.

———. *Non-Violence in Peace and War*. Ahmedabad: Navajivan Publishing House, 1948.

Goldfield, David R., *Black, White, and Southern: Race Relations and Southern Culture, 1940 to the Present*, Baton Rouge: Louisiana State University Press, 1991.

Gorky, Maxim, Alexander Kuprin, and I.A. Bunin. *Reminiscences of Anton Chekhov*. S. S. Koteliansky and L. Woolf, tr. New York: Huebsch, 1921.

Graysmith, Robert. *Unabomber: A Desire to Kill*. Washington DC: Regnery, 1997.

Hallett, Vicky. "Parks for People–Olmsted turned landscape into architecture." *U.S. News and World Report*, June 30, 2003.

Harding, Walter, ed. *Thoreau as Seen by his Contemporaries*. New York: Dover, 1989.

———. *The Days of Henry Thoreau*. New York: Dover, 1992.

Hawthorne, Nathaniel. *Tales*. James McIntosh, ed. New York: Norton, 1987.

———. *The Portable Hawthorne*. Malcolm Cowley, ed. New York: Viking, 1974.

Haynes, John Earl, and Harvey Klehr. *Early Cold War Spies: The Espionage Trials that Shaped American Politics*. Cambridge: Cambridge University Press, 2006.

Highsmith, Patricia. *The Talented Mr. Ripley*. New York: Random House / Vintage, 1992.

Hiss, Tony. *The View from Alger's Window: A Son's Memoir*. New York: Knopf, 1999.

Hoffman, Bruce. *Inside Terrorism*. New York: Columbia University Press, 1998.

Hofstadter, Douglas. *Gödel, Escher, Bach: An Eternal Golden Braid*. New York: Basic Books, 1999.

Hyman, Stanley Edgar. "Henry Thoreau in Our Time." In Sherman Paul, ed., *Thoreau: A Collection of Critical Essays,* Englewood Cliffs: Prentice-Hall, 1962, 23–36.

Idol, John L. Jr., and Buford Jones, eds. *Nathaniel Hawthorne: the Contemporary Reviews*. Cambridge and New York: Cambridge University Press, 1994.

Joyce, James. *Dubliners*. New York: Penguin, 1987.

Jung, Carl G. "On the Psychology of the Trickster Figure." In *Collected Works*, Princeton University Press, 1968, vol. 9, pt. 1, 3–41.

Kakutani, Michiko. "A Radical on the Run, Determined to Escape the Past." *New York Times*, Feb. 3, 2006.

Kalfus, Melvin. *Frederick Law Olmsted: The Passion of a Public Artist*. New York: New York University Press, 1990.

Kaufman, Gershen. *Shame: The Power of Caring*. Cambridge: Shenkman, 1985.

Kazdin, Andrew. *Glenn Gould at Work: Creative Lying*. New York: Dutton, 1989.

Kurtz, Michele. "The 'Stalker' who Stayed at Home: A Town Terrorized over the Internet." *Boston Globe*, Sept. 2, 2001.

Lebeaux, Richard. *Young Man Thoreau*. Amherst: University of Massachusetts Press, 1977.

Levin, Gail. *Edward Hopper: an Intimate Biography*. New York: Knopf, 1995.

Levin, Harry. *James Joyce*. New York: New Directions, 1960.

Lewin, Bertram. "Obsessional Neurosis." In Sándor Lorand, ed., *Psychoanalysis Today: Its Scope and Function*. New York, Covici-Friede, 1933, 266.

Lucie-Smith, Edward. *Lives of the Great 20th-century Artists*. London, Thames & Hudson, 1999.

Macalpine, Ida, and Richard Alfred Hunter. *Schizophrenia 1677: a Psychiatric Study of an Illustrated Autobiographical Record of Demoniacal Possession*. London: Dawson, 1956.

Magalaner, Marvin. *Time of Apprenticeship: the Fiction of Young James Joyce*. Freeport NY: Books for Libraries, 1970.

Marshall, Megan. *The Peabody Sisters: Three Women Who Ignited American Romanticism*. New York: Houghton Mifflin, 2005.

McGreevy, John, ed. *Glenn Gould by Himself and his Friends*. Toronto: Doubleday, 1983.

Mellow, James R. *Nathaniel Hawthorne in His Times*. Boston: Houghton Mifflin, 1980.

Melville, Herman. *Moby-Dick, or, the Whale*. New York: Penguin, 2003.

———, *Piazza Tales*. Egbert S. Oliver, ed. New York: Hendricks House, Farrar Straus, 1948.

Mendelsohn, Daniel. "An Affair to Remember." *New York Review of Books*, Feb. 23, 2006.

Moldenhauer, Joseph J. "Paradox in *Walden*." In Richard Ruland, ed., *Twentieth Century Intrpretations of* Walden, Englewood Cliffs, Prentice-Hall, 1968, 73–84.

Murray, Henry A. "American Icarus." In *Endeavors in Psychology*. E. S. Shneidman, ed. New York: Harper and Row, 1981, 535–56.

———. "Notes on the Icarus Syndrome." *Folia Psychiatrica, Neurologica et Neurochirurgica*, 61:42, 1958, 140–44.

Murry, John Middleton. *Fyodor Dostoevsky, a Critical Study*. New York: Russell & Russell, 1966.

Oates, Stephen B. *Let the Trumpet Sound: the Life of Martin Luther King, Jr.* New York: New American Library, 1982.

Olmsted, Frederick Law. *Creating Central Park, 1857–1861*, Baltimore: Johns Hopkins University Press, 1983, reprinted as vol. 3 of *The Papers of Frederick Law Olmsted*.

———. *Masterlist of Design Projects of the Olmsted Firm, 1857–1950*. Boston: Mass. Association of Parks, 1987.

———. *The Papers of Frederick Law Olmsted, Supplementary Series I: Writings on Public Parks, Parkways, and Park Systems*. Baltimore: Johns Hopkins University Press, 1997.

———. "The People's Park at Birkenhead, near Liverpool," *The Horticulturist*, May 1851.

Olmsted, F. L., Jr., and T. Kimball, eds., *Frederick Law Olmsted, Landscape Architect, 1833–1903*. New York: Putnam's, 1922.

Ostow, M. "The metapsychology of autoscopic phenomena." *Int. J. Psycho-anal.*, 1960, 41, 619–625.

Payzant, Geoffrey. *Glenn Gould: Music and Mind*. Toronto: Van Nostrand, 1997.

Proulx, Annie. *Brokeback Mountain*. New York: Scribner, 1997

Pushkin, Aleksandr. "The Shot." I. Keane, tr. In *Poems, Prose and Plays of Alexander Pushkin*, Avram Yarmolinksy, ed. New York: Modern Library, 1936.

Reich, Annie. "Narcissistic Object Choice in Women." In *Psychoanalytic Contributions*. New York: International Universities Press, 1953, 179–209.

Roper, Laura Wood. *FLO: A biography of Frederick Law Olmsted*. Baltimore: Johns Hopkins University Press, 1973.

Rybczynski, Witold. *A Clearing in the Distance: Frederick Law Olmsted and America in the Nineteenth Century*. New York: Scribner, 1999.

Sanborn, Franklin B. *The Life of Henry David Thoreau*. Boston: Houghton Mifflin, 1917.

Silva, J. Arturo, M.M. Ferrari, and G.B. Leong, "Asperger's disorder and the origins of the Unabomber." *American Journal of Forensic Psychiatry*, 2003, 24:2:5–43.

Simmons, Ernest J. *Feodor Dostoevsky*. New York: Columbia University Press, 1969.

Sperber, Michael A. *Henry David Thoreau: Cycles and Psyche*. Higganum CT: Higganum Hill Books, 2004.

Thoreau, Henry David. *Correspondence*. Carl Bode and Walter Harding, eds. Westport CT: Greenwood Press, 1958.

——— *Journal*. Bradford Torrey and Francis Allen, eds. 14 vols. New York: Dover, 1962.

———. *Reform Papers*. W. Glick, ed. Princeton: Princeton University Press, 1973.

———. *Walden*. J. L. Shanley, ed. Princeton: Princeton University Press, 1971.

Thurber, James. *The Secret Lives of Walter Mitty and of James Thurber*. New York: Harper Collins, 2006.

Todd, J., and K. Dewhurst. "The double: its psycho-pathology and psycho-physiology." *J. Nerv. Ment. Dis.*, 1955, 122(1):47–55.

Tolstoy, Leo. *Master and Man and Other Stories*. Ronald Wilks and Paul Foote, tr. New York: Penguin, 2005.

———. *What is Art?* Richard Pevear and Larissa Volokhonsky, tr. New York: Penguin Books, 1995.

Wallas, Graham. *The Art of Thought*. New York: Harcourt, Brace and Co., 1926.

Wasiolek, Edward. *Dostoevsky: the Major Fiction*. Cambridge: M.I.T. Press, 1964.

Williams, William Carlos. *Autobiography*. New York: New Directions, 1967.

Wineapple, Brenda. *Hawthorne: A Life*. New York: Random House, 2003.

Wotiz, John H., ed. *The Kekulé Riddle: a Challenge for Chemists and Psychologists*. Clearwater, FL: Cache River Press, 1993.

FILMS

Brokeback Mountain. Universal, 2005. With Heath Ledger and Jake Gyllenhaal. Directed by Ang Lee. Written by Larry McMurtry, based on a story by E. Annie Proulx.

Catch Me if You Can. Dreamworks, 2003. With Leonardo DiCaprio. Directed by Steven Speilberg. Written by Jeff Nathanson, based on Abagnale 1980.

The Talented Mr. Ripley. Paramount, 1999. With Matt Damon. Directed and written by Anthony Minghella, based on Highsmith 1955.

Zelig. 1983. With Woody Allen. Directed and written by Allen.

Index